MORITURI

MORITURI

THREE ONE-ACT PLAYS

TEJA — FRITZCHEN — THE ETERNAL MASCULINE

BY

HERMANN SUDERMANN

TRANSLATED FROM THE GERMAN

BY

ARCHIBALD ALEXANDER

CHARLES SCRIBNER'S SONS
NEW YORK :::::::::::::::::::::::::: 1917

CONTENTS

I

TEJA

A DRAMA IN ONE ACT

PERSONS

TEJA, King of the Goths.

BALTHILDA, Queen.

AMALABERGA, her mother.

AGILA, Bishop.

EURIC
THEODEMIR } Lords in the former king-
ATHANARIC } dom of the Goths.

ILDIBAD, spearbearer of the King.

HARIBALT, a warrior.

TWO CAMP WATCHERS.

TEJA

The scene represents the King's tent. The curtains are open in the background and permit a view through the camp of the Gothic warriors, over toward Vesuvius, and the distant sea, which shine in the splendour of the setting sun. On the left stands the rudely constructed throne of the King. In the centre, a table with seats around it. On the right, the King's couch, consisting of skins pieced together; above, a rack holding many kinds of weapons. Link torches on the right and left.

FIRST SCENE.

TWO CAMP WATCHERS.

FIRST CAMP WATCHER.

Ho thou! Art thou fallen asleep?

SECOND CAMP WATCHER.

Why should I be fallen asleep?

FIRST CAMP WATCHER.

Because thou leanest so limber upon thy spear, bent like the bow of a Hun.

Second Camp Watcher.

I stand so bent, because thus hunger gripes me less.

First Camp Watcher.

'Tis of no avail. It availeth as little as thy belt. Afterward, in standing upright, it is the more severe.

Second Camp Watcher.

How long is this to last?

First Camp Watcher.

Until the ships come—that is simple indeed.

Second Camp Watcher.

Yea, but when are the ships coming?

First Camp Watcher.

How can I know that? Look toward the heights. There, high upon the Milchberg, there standeth the watch, and overlooketh the sea for twenty miles. If he knoweth not! There, behind the Misenian hills, there they must be coming.

Second Camp Watcher.

Verily, if the Byzantian let them pass.

First Camp Watcher.

The Byzantian hath no ships.

SECOND CAMP WATCHER.

The Byzantian hath so many ships that he can surround the whole Italian world with them as with a hedge; as close as the Byzantian Eunuch hath surrounded us, these seven weeks.

FIRST CAMP WATCHER.

These seven weeks!

SECOND CAMP WATCHER.

Knowest thou what I got for nourishment, at noon this day? The same rind of bacon on which I brake my teeth eight days ago. Forsooth, I had cut my three crosses, with my knife. That was a meeting again! But to-day, I devoured it . . . a noble feast for a king's marriage day!

FIRST CAMP WATCHER.

Think'st thou the King had more?

SECOND CAMP WATCHER.

And think'st thou we would suffer ourselves to be beaten to death, suffer ourselves to be broken on the wheel, to be thrust through and put to shame, if he had more than we? Think'st thou we would lie here like chained dogs, and watch, did we not know that there is nothing to watch?

FIRST CAMP WATCHER.

There is gold enough.

[5]

SECOND CAMP WATCHER.

Gold! Pah, gold! Of gold I have enough myself. In my cellar at Canusium, I have buried a treasure—eh! . . . thou! The wives behind there in the Wagenburg must have meat left . . . wine too, they must still have.

FIRST CAMP WATCHER.

Yea, the wives are there well enough—thou hast none, I suppose.

SECOND CAMP WATCHER.

A Greek dishonoured mine, and I stabbed him to death! (*Pauses.*) Good! The wives must have meat; they must have wine too. But how long that— (*Noise and clash of weapons, slowly approaching.*) There, the marriage is surely ended.

FIRST CAMP WATCHER.

Silence! There cometh the aged Ildibad—with the King's shield. (*Both put themselves on guard.*)

SECOND SCENE.

THE SAME. ILDIBAD.

ILDIBAD.

(*Hangs the shield in its place, and puts away the weapons lying about.*) Hath any news been sent down?

[6]

T E J A

FIRST CAMP WATCHER.

Nay!

ILDIBAD.

Are ye hungry?

SECOND CAMP WATCHER.

Oh, yea.

ILDIBAD.

Hunger is for women—mark ye that! And show not such dark faces to our young Queen. That becometh not a marriage day.

THIRD SCENE.

Surrounded by noisy people, TEJA *and* BALTHILDA *have appeared in front of the tent. They enter led by* BISHOP AGILA. *Before them, two choir-boys swinging censers. Behind them,* AMALABERGA, EURIC, ATHANARIC, THEODEMIR, *and other lords and military leaders. The tent covers are let down. Exeunt the watchers.*

(BISHOP *lets go the hands of the bridal pair, and turns back to* AMALABERGA.)

(TEJA *stands gloomy and brooding.* BALTHILDA *casts a shy imploring look around her. Painful silence.*)

[7]

TEJA

ILDIBAD (*softly*).

Now must thou say something, King, to welcome thy young wife.

TEJA (*softly*).

Must I? (*Taking one of the choir-boys by the nape of the neck.*) Not so vehemently, boy; the smoke cometh up into our nostrils. What dost thou when thou wieldest not thy censer?

BOY.

I wield my sword, King.

TEJA.

That is right. But make ye haste with wielding the sword, or ye may easily be too late. (*Softly.*) Nothing to be seen of the ships, Ildibad?

ILDIBAD.

Nothing, my King. But thou must speak to thy young wife.

TEJA.

Yea . . . so now I have a wife, Bishop?

BISHOP.

Here standeth thy wife, King, and waiteth on thy word.

TEJA.

Forgive me, Queen, if I find not this word. I have been brought up in the midst of battles, and other dwelling-

[8]

place have I not known. It will be hard for thee to share this with me.

BALTHILDA.

King . . . my mother . . . taught me . . . (*She stops.*)

TEJA (*with assumed kindness*).

And what taught thee thy mother?

AMALABERGA.

That a wife belongeth to her husband—above all, in the hour of distress; she taught her that, King.

TEJA.

That may indeed be true and holy to ye wives. . . . If only the husband also belonged to his wife in the hour of distress. And yet one thing, Amalaberga. It hath been told me that in the morning, cocks crow near ye wives yonder in the Wagenburg. For weeks, the warriors have eaten no meat. I counsel ye, give them the cocks. (AMALABERGA *bows.*)

BISHOP.

My King!

TEJA.

Heh! Thou hast but now spoken so beautifully at the field-altar, Bishop. Dost thou desire to preach so soon again?

[9]

TEJA

BISHOP.

I will speak to thee, because bitterness devoureth thy soul.

TEJA.

Verily? Thou thinkest it? Then I give ear.

BISHOP.

Behold, like the spirit of divine wrath, so hast thou risen up among us, young man. . . . Not thy years did the nation count, only thy deeds. . . . Old men bowed willingly to thy youth, and since thou hadst yet a long time to serve, as one of the humblest, wert thou already our ruler. From the golden throne of Theoderic, where mercy had sat in judgment, where Totilas bestowed pardon with a smile, rang out sternly thy bloody word . . . And woe clave to us as a poisoned wound. . . . Pursued hither and thither beneath the hot outpourings of Vesuvius, we are now encamped with women and children; while Byzantium, with its hireling soldiers, holdeth us surrounded.

TEJA.

That it surely doth, ha, ha! Not a mouse can come through.

BISHOP.

Our gaze wandereth wistfully seaward: for thence hath God promised us bread.

TEJA

TEJA.

No tidings of the ships?

ILDIBAD (*softly*).

Nothing.

BISHOP.

Before we armed ourselves for a new war with misery, as free men, true to the ancient law, we determined to choose thee a wife, for in his own body should the King taste why the Goth loveth death.

TEJA.

Found ye that your King loved life overmuch?

BISHOP.

My King!

TEJA.

Nay, that dared ye not, for every hour of this life would hold ye up to mockery. . . . And even if the ancient law required it, why must ye weld me with this young thing which, trembling for fear before me and ye, hideth in her mother's skirts? And especially on so fitting a day, when hunger doth furnish the marriage music. . . . Look upon me, Queen—I must call thee by thy title of a half-hour, for, by God! I hardly yet know thy name. I pray thee, look upon me! Dost thou know me?

BALTHILDA.

Thou art the King, Sire.

Teja.

Yea. But for thee I should be man, not King. . . .
And knowest thou what manner of man standeth here
before thee? . . . Behold! These arms have been hitherto
plunged in reeking blood, not the blood of men shed in
manly strife, I speak not of that, that honoureth the man—
blood of unarmed pale children, of—(*shudders*)—Thou
shalt have great joy, if I come with these arms to wind
them about thy neck. . . . Dost thou indeed hear me?
Have I not a beautiful voice, a sweet voice? Only it
is a little hoarse. It is weary with screaming loud commands to murder. . . . Peculiar pleasure shall be thine
when thou hearest tender words with this bewitching
hoarseness. Am I not truly a born lover? These wise
men knew that; therefore they taught me my calling.
. . . Or believe ye, it was your duty to beguile your King
in the weariness of camp life; as the great Justinian dallied
in golden Byzantium, and sent forth his eunuchs to slay
Gothic men? Ha, ha, ha!

Bishop.

My King, take heed lest thou be angry.

Teja.

I thank thee, friend. Yet that signifieth nothing. It
is but my marriage humour. . . . But now I will speak to

[12]

ye in earnest—(*Ascends to the high seat of the throne.*)
On the golden throne of Theoderic, where mercy sat in
judgment, can I, alas! not take my place; for that is being
chopped into firewood at Byzantium. . . . Neither smiling like Totilas can I pardon, for no one longer desireth
our pardon. . . . From the glorious nation of the Goths,
there hath sprung a horde of hungry wolves—therefore it
needeth a wolf as master. Thou, Bishop, didst call me
the spirit of divine wrath, which I am not. . . . I am but
the spirit of your despair. As one who all his life hath
hoped for nothing, hath wished for nothing, I stand before
you, and so I shall fall before you. That ye knew, and
therefore ye are wrong, ye men, to reproach me secretly.
Contradict me not! . . . I read it clearly enough between
your lowering brows. . . . Because it goeth ill with us,
make not a scapegoat of me—that I counsel ye.

Theodemir.

King, wound us not. . . . The last drop of our blood
belongeth to thee. Cast us not into the pot with these
old men.

Euric.

We old men fight as well as they; and love, young man,
as well as they.

Teja.

Then let that suffice. Your Queen shall soon enough
learn how, in misfortune, friends quarrel among them-

selves. And as ye pass through the camp, tell the warriors, the only thing that frets the King this day—this day of joy, is it not?—is that he hath not the power to offer them a worthy marriage feast . . . or yet perchance— Ildibad.

ILDIBAD.

(*Who on the right has secretly spoken in bewilderment to a watcher who has just entered.*) Yea, Sire.

TEJA.

What have we still in our stores, old man?

ILDIBAD (*controlling his emotion*).

Truly, thou hast given away almost all thy provisions.

TEJA.

I ask thee, what remaineth?

ILDIBAD.

A jar of fermented milk, and two stale crusts of bread.

TEJA.

Ha, ha, ha! Now thou seest, Queen, what a poor husband thou hast got. Yet if the ships be there, as the people say, then will I do royal honours to every one, even as is his due. Yet tell it not, that would mar their joy. But if they hear the trumpets sound, then tell them there will be meat and wine on the long tables, so much as—

(*To* ILDIBAD, *who glides across the stage to his side*)
What is it?

ILDIBAD (*softly*).

The watch departeth. The ships are lost.

TEJA.

(*Without the least change of countenance.*) Lost—
how—in what way?

ILDIBAD.

Treason.

TEJA.

Yea, verily! Yea—meat and wine so much as each
one will, at long white tables—I shall have it divided—
and Sicilian fruits for the women, and sweetmeats from
Massilia. (*Sinks reeling upon the seat of the throne, and
gazes absently into the distance.*)

THE MEN.

What aileth the King? Look to the King!

BALTHILDA.

Surely he is hungry, mother. (*Approaches him. The
men draw back.*) My King!

TEJA.

Who art thou, woman? What wilt thou, woman?

BALTHILDA.

Can I help thee, Sire?

[15]

TEJA.

Ah, it is thou, the Queen! Pardon me; and pardon me, also, ye men. (*Rises.*)

BISHOP.

King, thou must husband thy strength.

THEODERIC.

Yea, King, for the sake of us all.

THE MEN.

For the sake of us all.

TEJA.

In truth, ye warn me rightly. Women, I pray ye, return to your encampment. We have to take counsel. Do thou, Bishop, see well to their safe conduct.

AMALABERGA (*softly*).

Make thy obeisance, child!

BALTHILDA (*softly*).

Mother, will he speak no more to me?

AMALABERGA.

Make thy obeisance! (*Balthilda obeys.*)

TEJA.

Fare ye well! (*Exeunt* BALTHILDA, AMALABERGA, BISHOP. *Shouts of applause without, greet them.*)

[16]

TEJA

FOURTH SCENE.

TEJA.   THEODEMIR.   EURIC.   ILDIBAD.   THE
WATCHER.   THE LORDS.

TEJA.

I have sent away the women and the priest; for what
comes now concerneth us warriors alone.   Where is the
watcher?   Come forth, man.

THE MEN (*muttering*).

The watcher from the hill!   The watcher!

TEJA.

Hereby ye know, men: the ships are lost.   (*Tumult.
Cries of horror.*)

TEJA.

Quiet, friends, quiet!   Thy name is Haribalt.

WATCHER.

Yea, Sire!

TEJA.

How long hast thou stood at thy post?

WATCHER.

Since early yesterday, Sire.

TEJA.

Where are thy two companions?

[17]

TEJA

WATCHER.

They remain above, as thou hast commanded, Sire.

TEJA.

Good, then what saw ye?

WATCHER.

The smoke of Vesuvius, Sire, descended upon the sea, beyond the promontory of Misenum. Thus we saw nothing until to-day about the sixth hour of the evening. Then suddenly the ships appeared—five in number— quite near the shore, there where it is said a city of the Romans lies buried in ruins. . . . One of us determined to hasten away, since——

TEJA.

Stay! What signal bare the ships?

WATCHER.

The foresail bound crosswise and——

TEJA.

And?

WATCHER.

A palm branch at the stern.

TEJA.

Ye saw the palm branch?

WATCHER.

As I see thee, Sire.

TEJA.

Good, go on.

WATCHER.

Then we perceived that the fishing-boats with which the Byzantians take their food, closely surrounded the ships, and then——

TEJA.

What then?

WATCHER.

Verily, Sire, they steered quite peaceably toward the camp of the enemy. There they unloaded. (*The men cover their heads. Silence.*)

TEJA.

(*Who looks, smiling, from one to the other.*) It is good. . . . That is: thou shalt say nothing there without. . . . From me they should learn it. (*Exit Watcher.*)

FIFTH SCENE.

TEJA. THEODEMIR. EURIC. ATHANARIC *and the* OTHERS. LORDS.

TEJA.

Your counsel, ye men!

[19]

TEJA

THEODEMIR.

Sire, we have none to give.

TEJA.

And thou, Euric, with all thy wisdom?

EURIC.

Sire, I have served the great Theoderic. And yet he would have had none to give.

TEJA.

Come then, I know. . . . It is easy and quick to be understood: Die! . . . Why look ye at me with such mistrust? . . . Do ye not yet understand me? Think ye I require ye to wrap yourselves in your mantles, like cowardly Greeks, and beg your neighbours for a thrust in the back? Be calm: I will protect you against shame, since I can no more lead you to honour.—Our place here cannot be taken, so long as thirty of us have power to wield our spears. But the hour shall come—and at no distant time—when the last arm, crippled by hunger, can no more be outstretched to beg quarter of the invading murderers.

THEODEMIR.

No Gothic man doeth that, King!

TEJA

TEJA.

For what thou art, thou canst give surety; for what thou shalt become, thou givest no surety to me. So I counsel and command ye to prepare yourselves for the last conflict. In the first gray of the morning, we shall burst forth from the clefts, and array ourselves against the Byzantian in open field.

ALL.

Sire, that is impossible.

THEODEMIR.

King, consider, we are one against a hundred.

TEJA.

And thou, Euric?

EURIC.

Sire, thou leadest us to destruction.

TEJA.

Yea, verily. Said I anything else? Do ye believe me to be so untried in things of war that I know not that? Why then halt ye? When Totilas led us, we were more than a hundred thousand. Now we are but five.—They all knew how to die, and can we, a miserable remnant, have forgotten it?

ALL.

Nay, King, nay!

TEJA

EURIC.

Sire, grant us time to accustom ourselves to that horrible thing.

TEJA.

Horrible? What seemeth horrible to ye? I speak not indeed to Romans who reel from the mass to the lupanar, and from the lupanar to the mass. Yet there is not one among ye whose breast is not covered with scars like an old stone with moss. These twenty years ye have made sport of death, and now it cometh in earnest, doth a Gothic man speak of "horrible"? What will ye? Will ye lie and hunger? Will ye devour one the other, like rats? Good. But I shall not do it with ye! Not I! To-morrow, I take spear and shield, and go to gain on my own account the bit of death for which I long and languish like a thief since ye made me leader of your lost cause.—And thou at least, my old companion, thou comest with me—eh?

ILDIBAD (*falling down before him*).

I thank thee, Sire! Why ask whether I come!

ALL.

We too, King. We all, we all!

[22]

TEJA

THEODEMIR.

Thou shouldst be praised, King, that thou hast pointed
to us the way of happiness. And be not angry with us,
if we were not able straightway to follow thee. Now I
perceive clearly thy great thought. From grief and dis-
cord and despair, we rise, we do not go down to death.
. . . Laughing, treadeth each on the other's corpse, in
order laughing to sink down like him. . . . A light will
go forth from us over the wide world. . . . Ah, that will
be a draught from golden goblets—that will be a riot of
exultant joy. Thank thee, my King. Often have I
envied thee thy crown, now I venture to envy it no
more.

TEJA.

The thing will come to pass for the most part otherwise
than thou dost imagine it, Theodemir. Yet I am glad
that among the Goths, such inspiration still abideth.

EURIC.

Also to me, King, grudge not a word; for I have indeed
seen golden days. . . . Thou art not only the boldest,
thou art also the wisest of all. . . . Had we now faltered,
so should we all have fallen without defence, by the
murderer's sword . . . And not only we, but the sick—and
the children—and the wives.

[23]

TEJA.

Ay, indeed, the wives! Of them I had not thought at all.

EURIC.

But now to-morrow, we shall stand in battle, and on the second and third day, if we hold out so long, so that astonishment and fear at the miracle will lay hold on the Byzantian and all the rabble of Huns and Suevians which he draggeth after him. . . . We cannot utterly destroy them, but we can bait them with our blood till they be weary. . . . And when no one on that side is able to hold spear and bow, then shall the hour come when the Eunuch will have it said: "Depart in peace." How many of ye are then still left?—I fear not many——

TEJA (*laughing*).

We, surely not!

ALL (*with cruel laughter*).

Nay, we surely not!

EURIC.

Then shall they take wives and children into the midst of them, and, head high, with naked swords, descend straight through the Byzantian camp toward Naples, to buy a piece of bread. And I tell ye, with such fear shall they be gazed at, that not even once shall a dog of the Huns dare to bark at them.

TEJA

Wife and child! Wife and child! What have we to do with them?

ATHANARIC.

King, thou revilest the dearest of our possessions.

TEJA.

Maybe!—I know only that there were too many mouths in the morning when the rations were divided. Otherwise we might have been able to support ourselves. And yet, this one thing I say to ye—and I shall enjoin it on the men without, upon their word as warriors—that none of the women know aught of our purpose. I will not that even one man be softened by the tears and cries of women.

ATHANARIC.

Sire, that is inhuman which thou requirest, to take no leave of our wives.

TEJA.

Take leave of them, me notwithstanding, but remain dumb as ye do it. He that hath wife and child here, let him go to the Wagenburg, and provide himself food and drink, for the women delight to keep a remnant between their fingers. This let him share with the unmarried, and be joyful when he can.

[25]

TEJA

EURIC.

And what should they say to their wives, Sire, since already thou hast strictly forbidden communication?

TEJA.

Say ye, it happens because of my marriage! Or the ships are there, if that sounds more worthy of belief. Say what ye will. Only that one thing, keep for yourselves.

THEODEMIR.

And wilt thou thyself nevermore see thy young wife?

TEJA.

Eh? Nay. . . . I mark not the least desire to. Surely now I shall speak to the people. I would that I had thy tongue, Theodemir.—The errand is troublesome to me, for I should speak great words, and I feel them not. Come! (*Exeunt all, with* ILDIBAD *slowly following.*)

SIXTH SCENE.

The stage remains unoccupied for a short time.—The voice of the King is heard, who is received with acclamation. Then after a few seconds, subdued cries of woe. ILDIBAD *returns and sits down upon a stump near the curtain. Then he lights two torches which he puts into the links, and prepares the weapons of the King. Outside arises a shout of enthusiasm, which again is subdued.*

TEJA

SEVENTH SCENE.

ILDIBAD. BISHOP AGILA (*tottering in with exhaustion and excitement*).

ILDIBAD.

Wilt thou not be seated, most worthy lord?

BISHOP.

And goest thou not to hear what the King saith?

ILDIBAD.

That hath naught to do with me, most worthy lord. The King and I—for a long time, we are united in action.

BISHOP.

Verily, he standeth there like the angel of death.

ILDIBAD.

Whether angel or devil, it is the same for me. (*The shout of enthusiasm rises anew and approaches the tent.*)

EIGHTH SCENE.

THE SAME. THE KING (*with flaming eyes, pale yet calm*).

TEJA

Are the weapons in order?—Ah, 'tis thou, Bishop!

BISHOP.

King, my King!

[27]

TEJA.

Surely, thou shalt now be driven to seek another flock, Bishop. Wilt thou but give me thy blessing, pray give it quickly. . . . Theodemir is about to come.

BISHOP.

And dost thou know thyself to be free, my son, from the trembling of every dying creature?

TEJA.

Bishop, I have been a good servant of thy church. To dedicate her temples, as once Totilas did, have I not been able; but what there was to kill, I have killed for her welfare. Shall I perform a posture for the blessed Arius?

BISHOP.

My son, I understand thee not.

TEJA.

For that I am sorry, my father.

BISHOP.

And hast thou taken leave?

TEJA.

Leave—of whom? Rather have I a mind to cry "welcome"; but yet nothing is there!

[28]

BISHOP (*indignantly*).

I speak of thy wife, Sire.

TEJA.

At this hour, I know only men, Bishop. Of wives I know nothing. Farewell! (*Enter* THEODEMIR *and* ILDIBAD.)

BISHOP.

Farewell—and God be gracious to thy soul!

TEJA.

I thank thee, Bishop. . . . Ah, there art thou, Theodemir. (*Exit* BISHOP AGILA.)

NINTH SCENE

TEJA. THEODEMIR. ILDIBAD (*in the background, occupied with the King's weapons, going noiselessly in and out*).

TEJA.

What are the warriors doing?

THEODEMIR.

They who have their wives here, are gone to the Wagenburg. . . . There they will surely eat and drink and play with their children.

TEJA.

And is thy wife here also?

[29]

THEODEMIR.

Yea, Sire!

TEJA.

And thy children?

THEODEMIR.

Two boys, Sire!

TEJA.

And thou didst not go?

THEODEMIR.

I waited on thy call, Sire.

TEJA.

What hour is it?

THEODEMIR.

The ninth, Sire.

TEJA.

And what do they who are free—the unmarried, and they whose wives are not here?

THEODEMIR.

They lie by the fires and are silent.

(*Exit* ILDIBAD.)

TEJA.

See to it that something is brought to them also. I already ordered it. Will they sleep?

[30]

TEJA

THEODEMIR.

No one will sleep.

TEJA.

At midnight, come and fetch me.

THEODEMIR.

Yea, Sire. (*Makes as if to go.*)

TEJA (*with a shade of anxiety*).

Theodemir, stay! . . . Thou hast always been my adversary.

THEODEMIR.

I was, Sire. For a long time I have ceased to be.

TEJA (*stretches out his arms*).

Come! (*They hold each other in a close embrace; then they clasp hands.*) I would fain hold thee here, but truly thou must go to thy wife. (ILDIBAD *again enters.*) And forget not to have food brought to those who are gazing at the fires. They should have occupation. Brooding profiteth not in such an hour.

THEODEMIR.

Yea, Sire. (*Exit.*)

TEJA

TENTH SCENE.

TEJA. ILDIBAD.

TEJA.

Now, my old man, we should have nothing further to do upon this earth.   Shall we talk?

ILDIBAD.

Sire, if I might beg a favour for myself.

TEJA.

Still favours, at this time? . . . I believe thou wouldst flatter me, old companion!

ILDIBAD.

Sire, I am old. My arm would grow weary with bearing a spear, more quickly than is good for thy life. And by my fault shouldst thou not fall, Sire. . . . If no one else sleeps, think not evil of me, and let me sleep away the two hours.

TEJA.

(*With a new gleam of deep anxiety.*)   Go, but not far away.

ILDIBAD.

Surely, Sire, I have always lain as a dog before thy tent. In respect of that, on this last night, nothing will be changed. . . . Hast thou orders to give, Sire?

TEJA

Good-night! (*Exit* ILDIBAD.)

ELEVENTH SCENE.

TEJA. *Afterward* BALTHILDA. (TEJA *left alone, throws himself on his couch, staring straight before him with a bitter, wearied smile.* BALTHILDA *enters shyly. In one hand she carries a basket containing meat, bread, and fruits; in the other, a golden tankard of wine. She advances a few steps toward the table.*)

TEJA (*half rising*).

Who art thou?

BALTHILDA (*feebly and timidly*).

Knowest thou me not, King?

TEJA (*rising from his couch*).

The torches burn dimly. . . . Thy voice I have heard before! . . . What wilt thou of me?

BALTHILDA.

I am indeed thy wife, King.

TEJA (*after a silence*).

And what wilt thou of me?

[33]

TEJA

BALTHILDA.

My mother sendeth me. I am to bring thee food and wine. The others eat and drink, and so my mother saith—— (*She stops.*)

TEJA.

How didst thou enter here? . . . Did not the watch forbid thee to enter?

BALTHILDA (*drawing herself up*).

I am the Queen, Sire.

TEJA.

Yea, verily. And Ildibad, what said he?

BALTHILDA.

Thy old spearbearer lay and slept. I stepped across him, Sire.

TEJA.

I thank thee, Balthilda. . . . I am not hungry. I thank thee. (*Silence.* BALTHILDA *stands and looks tearfully at him.*)

TEJA.

I see, thou hast still a request to make of me. I pray thee, speak!

[34]

TEJA

BALTHILDA.

My King, if I return home with a well-filled basket, then shall I be mocked by all the women. . . . And the men shall say——

TEJA (*smiling*).

And what shall the men say?

BALTHILDA.

He esteemeth her so little that—he consenteth not to take food from her hand.

TEJA.

On my word, I assure thee, Balthilda, the men have other things to think on . . . yet nevertheless . . . reproach thou shalt not suffer through me. Set thy basket there. . . . Have ye still much of such things?

BALTHILDA.

Sire, these two weeks have my mother and I and the women about us put aside the best of our share—flour and fruits—and the fowls have we not killed till this very day.

TEJA.

Then indeed must ye have been mightily hungry, ye women?

TEJA

BALTHILDA.

Ah, it hath done us no hurt, Sire. . . It was for a feast.

TEJA.

In truth? Ye believed we should celebrate a feast to-day?

BALTHILDA.

Well . . . is it then not a feast, Sire?

TEJA.

(*Is silent and bites his nether lip, examining her furtively.*) Wilt thou not be seated, Balthilda? . . . I should not yet let thee go home! That too would be a reproach, would it not?

(BALTHILDA *is silent and looks down.*)

TEJA.

And if I bade thee, wouldst thou wish to stay?

BALTHILDA.

Sire, how should a wife not wish to stay beside her husband?

TEJA.

Hast thou then the feeling in thy heart, that I—am—thy—husband?

TEJA

BALTHILDA.

Indeed, how could it be otherwise? The Bishop hath joined us together.

TEJA.

And wert thou glad when he did it?

BALTHILDA.

Yea. . . . Nay, I was not glad then.

TEJA.

Why not?

BALTHILDA (*with a bright glance*).

Perhaps because, because . . . I was afraid, Sire, and I was praying.

TEJA.

What didst thou pray?

BALTHILDA.

That God would grant to me, his humble handmaid, the power to bring thee the happiness which thou needest, and which thou awaitest from me.

TEJA.

Which I from thee—that didst thou pray?

BALTHILDA.

Sire, may I not offer thee the food, and the wine?

TEJA.

Nay, nay! . . . Hearken, Balthilda: without, by our fires, are warriors—they are hungry—I am not hungry.

BALTHILDA.

Sire, give them what thou pleasest . . . give them everything!

TEJA.

I thank thee, Balthilda. (*Raising the curtain.*) Ho there, watch! Come in, but prudently so as not to wake the old man. . . . (*Watcher enters.*) Here, take this basket with food and wine, and divide it honestly. . . . Say your Queen sends it.

WATCHER.

May I thank the Queen, Sire?

(TEJA *nods.* WATCHER *shakes her hand heartily. Exit.*)

TEJA.

Go—and bring me to eat!

BALTHILDA (*perplexed*).

Sire—why—mockest thou—me?

TEJA.

Dost thou then not understand me? If thou wilt be my wife, thou must offer me my property, not thine!

[38]

TEJA

BALTHILDA.

Is not all of mine thy property, Sire?

TEJA.

Hm! (*Silence. He takes her hands.*) Call me not Sire and call me not King. . . . Knowest thou not my name?

BALTHILDA.

Thy name is Teja!

TEJA.

Say it yet once again!

BALTHILDA (*softly, turning away*).

Teja!

TEJA.

Is the name so strange to thee?

(**BALTHILDA** *shakes her head.*)

TEJA.

Then why hesitate?

BALTHILDA.

Not for that, Sire! Since I knew that I was to serve thee as thy wife, I have often named thee by day and in the night. Only I never said it aloud. . . .

TEJA.

And before thou knewest it, what was then thy thought?

[39]

BALTHILDA.

Sire, why dost thou ask?

TEJA.

And why dost thou not answer?

BALTHILDA.

Sire, when I heard of thy bloody commands, and the others feared thee—then I often thought: How unhappy must he be that the destiny of the Goths compelleth him to such deeds!

TEJA.

That hast thou thought?—That hast thou——?

BALTHILDA.

Sire, was it wrong that I should think it?

TEJA.

Thou hadst never seen my face, and thou didst understand me? And they who were around me, the wise men and tried soldiers, they understood me not! . . . Who art thou, woman? Who hath taught thee to read my heart?—Thee, thee alone of all?

BALTHILDA.

Sire—I——

[40]

TEJA

All shuddered and muttering hid themselves from me in corners—and saw not the way, the only way which haply might still have saved them. When the butcher's knife was already at their throat, they still told themselves some tale of compromise. And then came the crafty Greeks, measured themselves with them, and killed them one by one. Thus perished the hundred thousand. And I wrapped myself in grief and anger—I cast hope away from me like a bloody rag, I sprang into the breach with scornful laughter. I sowed horrors about me, when my own heart was convulsed with horror of myself. I have not once been drunk with all the blood. I have killed, killed, and still knew all the while: it is in vain! (*He sinks to his seat overcome with anguish, and stares straight before him.*)

BALTHILDA (*with a shy attempt at a caress*).

My poor dear King! Dear Teja!

TEJA.

(*Raises his head and looks confusedly around him.*) My God, what do I here? . . . Why do I tell all this to thee? Thou must not despise me because I am such a babbler. . . . Nor must thou believe that it is aught of remorse that compels me to this confession. . . . Perhaps I feel

[41]

pity for the victims, but my conscience stands high above all that! . . . Far higher than my poor Gothic throne. . . . Look not upon me so. . . . There is in thy eye something that compels me to reveal my inmost thought to thee. . . . Who hath endued thee with this power over me? . . . Begone! . . . Nay, stay . . . Stay! I wish to tell thee yet something, quite in secret, before thou goest. . . . Besides, I should not cry out so, otherwise the watch may hear. . . . Incline thine ear to me. Never yet have I confessed it to any man, nor have I held it possible that I should ever confess it. . . . I bear an envy within me which devoureth my heart, whenever I think—knowest thou toward whom? . . . Toward Totilas. . . . Yea, toward Totilas in his grave. . . . They called him the "shining" Totilas and their affection still cleaveth to him to-day. . . . Their eyes still flash when they even think of him.

BALTHILDA.

Ah, Sire, how thou dost fret thyself!

TEJA (*anxiously*).

Didst thou ever see him?

BALTHILDA.

Never.

TEJA.

God be thanked! For hadst thou ever seen him as I saw him on the morning of the battle in which he fell

. . . arrayed in golden armour . . . and the white steed pranced beneath him, and his yellow locks streamed like sunlight about him. And he laughed the foe in the face. . . . Laughed like a child! . . . Ah, laughing to die like him!

BALTHILDA.

His lot was easy, Sire! He went from hence, but left to thee as an inheritance the half-destroyed kingdom. . . . How shouldst thou then have laughed?

TEJA (*eagerly*).

Is it not so?—Is it not so?—How . . . Ah, that doeth good! (*Stretching himself.*) Ah, thou doest me good!

BALTHILDA.

How proud thou makest me, Sire!

TEJA.

But hadst thou seen him and compared him to me, thou wouldst spit upon me!

BALTHILDA (*fervently*).

I should have seen only thee, Sire—dear, dear Sire!

(TEJA *looks askance at her, shyly and distrustfully, then walks silently to the left, sinks down before the seat on the throne, and burying his face in the chair, weeps bitterly.*)

BALTHILDA.

(*Follows him shyly and kneels down beside him.*) Teja,
beloved, if I hurt thee, pardon me!

TEJA (*rises and grasps her arm*).

Tell it to no one!

BALTHILDA.

What, Sire?

TEJA.

That thou hast seen me weep! Swear it to me!

BALTHILDA.

It hath been told me that I am now even as a piece
of thy body—and of thy soul also! . . . Wherefore should
I swear?

TEJA.

If thou art a piece of my body, then come nearer to me,
that thou mayst not see my tears.

BALTHILDA.

Let me dry them for thee! See, for this cause am I
here.

TEJA.

Ah, 'tis well with me. . . . I must indeed have died
of shame, for never yet hath a Gothic man been seen to
weep. Even when we buried Totilas, we wept not. . . .

Yet I am not ashamed. . . . If I but knew why suddenly it is so well with me! . . . Balthilda, I will tell thee something. But thou must not laugh me to scorn.

BALTHILDA.

How should I laugh at thee, beloved?

TEJA.

I am hungry.

BALTHILDA (*springing up in surprise*).

Alas, surely thou hast given everything away!

TEJA.

Oh, by no means! Go just over there, wilt thou? (*She obeys.*) Behind my couch—seest thou the fireplace?

BALTHILDA.

Here where the ashes lie?

TEJA.

There standeth a chest?

BALTHILDA.

Yea.

TEJA.

Wilt thou open the lid?

BALTHILDA.

Ah, it is heavy!

[45]

TEJA

TEJA.

Now feel within! Deep, deep! . . . There Ildibad
the old miser—well?

BALTHILDA (*disappointedly*).

A couple of bread crusts; is that all, Sire?

TEJA.

There is indeed nothing more.

BALTHILDA.

May I not then go quickly over to the Wagenburg?
. . . Perhaps still . . .

TEJA.

Oh nay. . . . They themselves need the fragments.
. . . Bring that hither! As brothers we shall share it—
eh? And then there is sufficient for both. Wilt thou?

BALTHILDA.

Yea. (*She sits beside him.*)

TEJA.

So, now give to me! Ah, that is good to the taste!
Is it not good to the taste? But ah, thou also must eat.

BALTHILDA.

I fear there is not enough for thee.

TEJA.

Nay, that is against the agreement. . . . So. . . . Is it not good to the taste?

BALTHILDA.

To me nothing hath ever tasted half so sweet.

TEJA.

Pray come nearer to me . . . I will take the crumbs from thy lap . . . So—why is it that suddenly I am hungry? See, now we celebrate our marriage feast.

BALTHILDA.

And better than those without, with meat and wine— do we not?

TEJA.

Well, did I not tell thee? . . . But thou hast a bad seat!

BALTHILDA.

Nay, I am seated well!

TEJA.

Come, stand up! Pray, stand up!

BALTHILDA (*rising*).

Well?

TEJA

Sit there, just above!

[47]

BALTHILDA (*terrified*).

Upon the throne—for God's sake—how dare I——?

TEJA.

Art thou not then the Queen?

BALTHILDA (*decidedly*).

If I must sit there in earnest! But in jest—nay!

TEJA.

Ah, the stupid bit of wood! (*He hurls down the throne.*) At least it should be of use for something! . . . So now lean against it!

BALTHILDA.

Beloved, doest thou justly?

TEJA (*surprised*).

Nay! (*He sets the throne up again, leads her to her former place, and places her head against the seat.*) There indeed thou art well seated—yea! . . . And we trespass not against this trash. If the Bishop had seen that—he, ha, ha, ha! Wait, I will eat again!

BALTHILDA.

There, take!

TEJA.

Still—remain quite still! I shall fetch it for myself. (*He kneels upon the podium beside her.*) Now I am

quite upon my knees before thee. . . . What is there that
we do not learn! . . . Thou art beautiful! . . . I never
knew my mother!

BALTHILDA.

Never knew!

TEJA.

Never had a sister. . . . No one. . . . Never played
in my life. . . . That I am surely learning last not least.

BALTHILDA.

Why last not least?

TEJA.

Ask not—nay? Ah thou, thou! Ha, ha, ha! Pray
eat! Bite from mine—yea? Obediently—thou knowest
what the Bishop said?

BALTHILDA (*bites and then springs up*).

But wilt thou not also drink?

TEJA.

Ah, surely! Bring me only the milk jar! Bring me only
the milk jar. . . . Thou knowest the one that Ildibad
told us of.

BALTHILDA (*who has walked across*).

Is this the one?

[49]

TEJA

TEJA (*rising*).

That is indeed it. But thou also must drink.

BALTHILDA.

Is it fitting so?

TEJA.

I know not. It should be!

BALTHILDA.

So be it, then. (*She drinks and shakes with laughter.*)
Ugh! That hath a bad taste.

TEJA.

Give it to me. (*He drinks.*) Nay! (*He drinks
again.*) Go! . . . Art thou then such a despiser of
nourishment? . . . Yea, who art thou then? And how
comest thou hither? And just what wilt thou of me?

BALTHILDA.

I will love thee!

TEJA.

Thou—my wife! Thou . . . (*They fly into one another's arms. Softly.*) And wilt thou not kiss me?

(BALTHILDA *shakes her head, ashamed.*)

TEJA.

Why not?

TEJA

(BALTHILDA *again shakes her head.*)

TEJA.

Yet tell me, why not?

BALTHILDA.

I will tell thee in thine ear.

TEJA.

Well?

BALTHILDA.

Thou hast a downy beard.*

TEJA.

(*Wipes his mouth in terror, then in assumed anger.*)
What have I? Knowest thou not who I am? How then
dost thou suffer thyself to tell thy King he—say it yet
once more! I will but see.

BALTHILDA (*laughing*).

A—downy—beard.

TEJA (*laughing*).

Now, wait!

* Milchbart—literally " milky beard."

T E J A

THE SAME.   ILDIBAD.

ILDIBAD.

Sire, thou calledst? (*He stands rigid with astonishment, and is about to retire silently.*)

TEJA.

(*Collects himself abruptly. He appears to wake out of a dream. His manners and bearing revert to the gloomy energy which previously had the ascendency.*) Stop, stay, what happens without?

ILDIBAD.

The warriors return from the Wagenburg, sire, and most of the wives come with them.

TEJA.

Are the leaders assembled?

ILDIBAD.

Yea, Sire.

TEJA.

They might have patience for a moment more.

ILDIBAD.

Yea, Sire.

[52]

TEJA.

For I also have a wife.

ILDIBAD.

Yea, verily, Sire.

[*Exit.*]

THIRTEENTH SCENE.

TEJA.   BALTHILDA.

BALTHILDA.

Teja, beloved, what happeneth to thee?

TEJA.

(*Remains standing before her and takes her head in his hands.*)   To me, it is as if in this hour we had strayed hand in hand through a whole world of joy and sorrow. That disappeareth—all disappeareth. I am again the —I was—nay, I am not he.—But be thou high above all the women, the Queen . . . Wilt thou?

BALTHILDA.

Sire, what dost thou require of me?

TEJA.

Thou wilt not entreat and wilt not cry out?

BALTHILDA.

Nay, Sire.

[53]

TEJA

TEJA.

The day draweth nigh.   Before us standeth death.

BALTHILDA.

Sire, I understand thee not.   None can attack us, and until the ships come——

TEJA.

The ships come never more.

(BALTHILDA *strokes herself on the cheeks, and then stands motionless.*)

TEJA.

But we men are going forth upon the field, to fight.

BALTHILDA.

That can ye not do—that is surely—impossible.

TEJA.

We must.   Art thou the Queen, and perceivest not that we must?

BALTHILDA.

Yea—I—per—ceive—it.

TEJA.

The King fights in the foremost rank, and we shall see each other no more alive. . . . Knowest thou that?

BALTHILDA.

Yea, I know it! . . . (*Silence. They look at each other.*)

TEJA.

Thy blessing will I have upon the way. (*He sinks on his knees before her; she lays her hands upon his head, bends down to him, trembling, and kisses him on the forehead.*)

TEJA.

(*Springs up and tears back the curtain.*) Enter, who waiteth there!

FOURTEENTH SCENE.

THE SAME. AMALABERGA, EURIC, AGILA, ATHANARIC, THEODEMIR, *and other leaders.*

AMALABERGA.

King, I sent my child to thee. . . . I hear ye men have to act. . . . Give her again to me.

TEJA.

Here hast thou thy child! (*Exeunt* AMALABERGA *and* BALTHILDA.)

TEJA

THE SAME. *Except* AMALABERGA *and* BALTHILDA.

TEJA.

(*Stares after them, rouses himself, and perceives the Bishop.*) Bishop, I treated thee basely this evening. Forgive me and have my thanks, for surely I also know why the Goth loveth death. . . . (*Grasps his sword.*) Now be ye ready? Have the farewells been said?

THEODEMIR.

Sire, we have disobeyed thy command. Which of our wives betrayed it, and which of us told it, that cannot be determined. Enough, they all know it.

TEJA.

And then have cried ah and woe?

THEODEMIR.

Sire, they have silently kissed the blessing of death upon our brows.

TEJA (*exclaims half to himself*).

They also! (*Aloud.*) Truly we are a nation of kings. It is our misfortune. So come! (*He strides to the background. The others follow. Amid the noisy cries of the people greeting the King, the curtain falls.*)

[56]

II

FRITZCHEN

A DRAMA IN ONE ACT

PERSONS

HERR VON DROSSE, Major (retired), Lord of the Manor.

HELENE, his wife.

FRITZ, their son.

AGNES, niece of Frau von Drosse.

VON HALLERPFORT, lieutenant.

STEPHAN, overseer.

WILHELM, servant.

FRITZCHEN

*The action takes place on Herr von Drosse's estate.
Time, the present.*

*The scene represents a drawing-room on the ground
floor. In the rear are wide glass doors which stand open,
and permit a view of the terrace and splendid park lying
beyond. Windows to the right and left. On the right
side, a sofa with table and chairs; on the left, a secretary
with writing materials. Handsome old-fashioned decora-
tions, pictures of battles, portraits in oval frames, racing
prints, etc. The terrace is sheltered by a broad awning
which slightly subdues the glare of the bright summer
afternoon.*

FIRST SCENE.

WILHELM (*servant over sixty, in half livery, is engaged in arranging the samovar for the afternoon coffee*).
AGNES (*extremely slender, nervous, with traces of mental
distress—twenty years of age—blonde hair smoothed on the
temples, light muslin gown, a garden hat in her hand—
enters from the terrace*).

FRITZCHEN

AGNES.

Wilhelm, has the postman been here?

WILHELM (*sighing*).

Yes, yes, he was here.

AGNES.

Where are the things?

WILHELM.

They are on the table, Fräulein.

AGNES.

(*Goes quickly to the table and with feverish haste looks through the small pile of newspapers and letters lying there.*)   Again, nothing!

WILHELM.

Yes, indeed—and this is the seventh day. Ah, it is really heart-breaking.

AGNES.

Are your master and mistress still taking their after-noon nap?

WILHELM.

I have just heard the Major. He will be here directly —there he is now!

FRITZCHEN

SECOND SCENE.

THE SAME. MAJOR VON DROSSE (*about fifty, tall, broad-shouldered, rather stout. Dark-grayish full beard parted in the middle, waving right and left over his shoulders. In the full, well-browned face with flashing eyes and bushy eyebrows, there are energy and abundant vitality, controlled by the self-command and chivalric manner of an old officer. Brief in speech, domineering, but never without a gleam of inner kindness*).

MAJOR.

Afternoon, Agnes!

AGNES.

Afternoon, uncle!

MAJOR.

(*Goes to the table, examines the letters, sits down and looks straight before him for a little while.*)   Wilhelm!

WILHELM.

What does the Major wish?

MAJOR.

Stephan is to come at once to the castle.

WILHELM.

Very well, Major.   (*Exit.*)

FRITZCHEN

MAJOR.

Agnes, my child, just listen to me . . . You are a reasonable creature . . . One that I can talk to. . . . So the rascal has again not written. He should have come to us, day before yesterday. Has made no excuses—doesn't write—nothing. That has not happened during the six years that he has been away from home. I ordered him most strictly to send a letter, or at least a card, every day—for with her illness, your aunt must be guarded against the slightest anxiety or excitement. He knows that, and moreover has always observed it conscientiously. I can't any longer be responsible for your aunt and her weakened heart. Unless we use every means to keep her in her—visionary life, she will go to pieces.

AGNES.

Uncle!

MAJOR.

We must make up our minds to that, Agnes. Really, I do what I can. Yesterday I even forged a telegram to her—you know that, eh! I did intend to write to his intimate friend Hallerpfort, but thought better of it. I shall drive into town directly after dark. Without your aunt knowing it, of course—for now, during the harvest, that would upset her still more. So you will stay all

night with her, and er—well, the rest I will arrange with
Stephan.

AGNES.

Very well, dear uncle.

MAJOR.

Just come here, girl, look me in the face . . . We two
know each other and . . . Eh?

(AGNES *casts down her eyes.*)

MAJOR.

Now see, I know very well that for two years you have
been secretly corresponding with Fritz.

AGNES.

Uncle! (*Presses her hands to her face.*)

MAJOR.

There, that will do, that will do, that will do. . . . You
can well believe, if I had been opposed to it on principle,
I should have long since put an end to the business,
shouldn't I? . . . But there are things—well, in short,
that you don't understand. Well, I should not have
begun about the matter to-day, but necessity knows no
law, eh? And if I go to see him this evening, I don't
wish to grope altogether in the dark. . . . So—on the
basis of what has just been said—have you, perhaps, by
any chance had a letter from him?

FRITZCHEN

AGNES.

No, uncle!

MAJOR.

Hm!

AGNES (*hesitating, embarrassed*).

For some time we have not corresponded.

MAJOR.

So ?—Ho, ho . . .!—Who is to blame for that ?

AGNES.

Ah, let us not talk about that, uncle. But from another quarter, I have had news of him.

MAJOR.

When ?

AGNES.

Yesterday.

MAJOR.

And that you have——?

AGNES.

(*Taking a letter from her pocket.*) Please read—and I think you will not reproach me.

MAJOR (*unfolding the letter*).

Ah, from the little Frohn! Now then, what does the little Frohn write ? (*Reads, muttering.*) Lanskis—Stein-

[64]

hof—met cousin—danced (*aloud*).   Indeed, then he could dance, but not write, that is a nice business—I should not have believed it of him at all. . . . (*Reads further, muttering*.)   Eyes for the so-called beautiful Frau von Lanski . . . The whole regiment is talking of it. . . . Hm! eh, what!   Such a goose!   What things such a goose does cackle! . . . Regiment has other things to bother itself about. . . . But such a regulation goose . . . If a young lieutenant like that isn't all the time trotting after them. And when he once shows attention to a lady who doesn't belong to the regiment . . . Besides, the Lanski is nearly forty . . . Such idiocy!   Then he might at least—hm— hm—eh, pardon!   Now then, what is it? . . . My poor old girl . . . Yes, yes, jealousy . . . You have borne up disgracefully since yesterday.

AGNES.

I think I have controlled myself, uncle?

MAJOR.

Yes, very true, girl, no one has noticed anything.

THIRD SCENE.

THE SAME.   WILHELM.   *Afterward* STEPHAN, *the overseer*.

WILHELM (*entering from the right*).

Herr Stephan is there, Major.

FRITZCHEN

MAJOR.

Come in!

(*Enter* STEPHAN.)

Very well, my dear Stephan, I must drive into town directly after dark. Unless I should be detained, I shall be here early to-morrow morning—four and a half and four and a half more miles—nine miles. . . . The coach horses have been exercised to-day?

STEPHAN.

Yes, indeed, Major.

MAJOR.

Which are in better condition now, the browns or the whites?

STEPHAN.

That I don't permit myself to decide, Major. They have all had it severely!

MAJOR.

Well, I will just go and have a look myself. Wilhelm—cap!

WILHELM.

Very well, Major. (*Exit to the right.*)

MAJOR.

And at half after nine this evening, send a message to my wife and have her told that I must stay all night at the brick kilns—eh, you remember (*softly, looking around at* AGNES) how we managed it the other times when I was out at night.

STEPHAN.

All right, Major.

MAJOR.

Where is that fellow stopping with my cap? (*Enter* WILHELM.) Where were you hiding, man? (WILHELM *hands him the cap*.) And he is tottering on his old legs! What are you tottering so for?

WILHELM.

Indeed I am not tottering, Major.

MAJOR.

Well, come on, Stephan! (*Exeunt* MAJOR, STEPHAN, *through the garden door*.)

FOURTH SCENE.

AGNES. WILHELM. *Afterward* LIEUTENANT VON HALLERPFORT.

WILHELM (*softly*).

Fräulein, just now as I went out, Lieutenant von Hallerpfort was standing there and wished to speak with Fräulein, privately. Neither the master nor the mistress is to know anything of it . . . God, Fräulein is deadly pale!

FRITZCHEN

AGNES.

Ask the lieutenant to come in, and keep a lookout, if my aunt comes.

(WILHELM *opens the door on the right, and disappears through the door on the left hand.*)

AGNES.

(*Meeting the lieutenant as he enters.*) Herr von Hallerpfort, what has happened to Fritz?

HALLERPFORT.

Nothing, Fräulein, not the least thing. . . . I am surprised that he is not yet here.

AGNES (*rising joyfully*).

Ah! (*With a sigh of relief.*) Ha!

HALLERPFORT.

I beg pardon a thousand times if I startled you.

AGNES.

Will you please take a seat.

HALLERPFORT.

Thank you, most humbly! (*They are seated.*) Your uncle and aunt, I hope, will not——

FRITZCHEN

AGNES.

Uncle has just gone to the stables, and aunt's coming will be announced to us.

HALLERPFORT.

How is your aunt?

AGNES.

Oh, I thank you, much as usual.—Herr von Hallerpfort, be frank with me: What is this all about?

HALLERPFORT.

Oh, absolutely nothing of any consequence. A little surprise—nothing further—nothing further!

AGNES.

To be sure, if he is really on his way here—didn't you ride here together?

HALLERPFORT.

No, I came by the way of the levee, and thought to overtake him. He will have ridden by the highway.

AGNES.

Then what is the object of this secrecy?

HALLERPFORT.

That will soon be cleared up, Fräulein. . . . At this moment, in Fritz's interest, I have to ask a great favour of

[69]

you. . . . It is now (*takes out his watch*) three forty-five o'clock. At four o'clock—let us say five minutes after four —even if we take into account some unforeseen delay— yes—he must be here. . . . How long does it take to go to the village to Braun's inn?

AGNES.

Ten minutes—that is, by a short cut through the park, about five.

HALLERPFORT.

Thank you most humbly. Then will you have the great kindness to reckon by your watch a half hour from the moment when he comes in here, and then send me a message to Braun's where I am stopping?

AGNES.

At Braun's? I think you know, Herr von Hallerpfort, that this house——

HALLERPFORT.

Oh, certainly—that I know! . . . I only made the mistake of putting my horse at the entrance to Braun's, and as he doesn't belong to me, it is my duty to look after him.

AGNES.

And all that is the truth?

HALLERPFORT.

Absolutely.

AGNES.

I should not be so persistent—forgive me for it—but here we have all been so distressed about him. For nearly a week, we have sat and waited for news. . . . Tell me truly.

WILHELM (*entering at the left*).

Fräulein, your aunt.

HALLERPFORT (*springing up*).

Good-bye, then! And be reassured, it is all about a joke—about——

AGNES.

If only your face were not so serious.

HALLERPFORT.

Oh, that—that is deceptive. (*Exit quickly to the right.*)

FIFTH SCENE.

AGNES. FRAU VON DROSSE (*extremely delicate in appearance, forty, suffering—with girlish complexion—gay, absent smile—dreamy, gentle expression—gliding, careful walk—breathing deeply*).

AGNES.

(*Hastens to meet her, to support her.*) Forgive me, aunt, that I did not go to fetch you.

FRITZCHEN

FRAU VON DROSSE.

No matter, darling . . . I could manage. . . . Is there any news?

(AGNES *shakes her head.*)

FRAU VON DROSSE (*sighing*).

Ah, yes.

AGNES.

Do you know, aunt, I have a sort of presentiment that he will soon be here himself.

FRAU VON DROSSE.

Yes, if things happened according to presentiments!

SIXTH SCENE.

THE SAME. MAJOR. WILHELM.

MAJOR.

Well, darling, are you in good spirits? . . . No! . . . Well, what is it then? What is it then?

FRAU VON DROSSE.

Ah, Richard, you surely know.

MAJOR.

Oh, nonsense! Don't worry yourself uselessly. . . . A young badger like that—service and casino and what not! I used not to do any better myself . . . Eh, Wilhelm, that you will have remembered even in your booziness? Many a time I didn't write for four weeks.

WILHELM (*who is handing the coffee*).

Yes, Major.

MAJOR.

And were you at all worried then?

WILHELM.

Yes, Major.

MAJOR.

Old donkey. . . . Well, you see how it is . . . The same old story.

FRAU VON DROSSE.

Richard, do you know, last night a thought came to me. They all idolise him—that boy.

MAJOR.

Yes?

FRAU VON DROSSE.

Well, with the ladies of the regiment, it is no great wonder. . . .

MAJOR.

So far as they wish to get married—no.

[73]

FRITZCHEN

FRAU VON DROSSE.

But there is another who takes a very special interest in him—motherly, as one might say. . . . No; motherly is not just the right word, but at any rate, purely human, purely spiritual—you know what I mean. At the last ball in Wartenstein, she questioned me at length about him, about his childhood, and everything possible. At the time I was really rather indignant, but now it pleases me. . . . I shall write to her to-day and ask her to keep an eye upon him. For you see, a woman's influence—that is what he needs.

MAJOR.

Ah, the poor devil! And for that purpose, one of the kind. . . . Who then is it?

FRAU VON DROSSE.

Why! You surely know her . . . Frau von Lanski of Steinhof.

(AGNES *winces.*)

MAJOR.

Ah, indeed—well, to be sure, hm—that is quite probable.

FRAU VON DROSSE.

Their estate is quite close to the city . . . There he could always go in the evenings . . . If only the husband were not so rude. I should be afraid of him.

[74]

MAJOR.

Well, you are not a lieutenant of hussars, darling.

AGNES.

Won't you drink your coffee, aunt? It will be quite cold.

FRAU VON DROSSE.

Ah, the stupid fig-coffee. To be sure, your health is good, you don't need anything of the kind! (*drinks*) Richard, do you know, last night I saw a vision.

MAJOR.

Well, what did you see this time, darling?

FRAU VON DROSSE.

There was a wide chamber with many mirrors and lights—perhaps it was Versailles—perhaps the castle at Berlin. And hundreds of generals stood there and waited. . . . (*Excitedly.*) And suddenly the door was opened wide and at the side of the Emperor——

AGNES.

Drink, aunt—tell about it later—it excites you.

FRAU VON DROSSE.

Yes, my sweet one, yes. (*Drinks and leans back exhausted.*) You know, Richard, perhaps they are to increase his pay.

MAJOR.

Surely he has enough, darling. Do you wish him to gamble it away?

FRAU VON DROSSE.

Very well, then, let him gamble it away. I find that in general we pay so little heed to him . . . . I am obliged to think all the time how he acted in a roundabout way in the matter of Foxblaze. He didn't trust himself even to tell it.

MAJOR (*laughing*).

No, child—but just stop. . . . Besides the charger he already has two others . . . And one of them is Mohammed! Such a big stable—it is only a nuisance to him. . . . Just consider!

FRAU VON DROSSE.

Ah, it is surely only restlessness. Ah, I wish he were only——

WILHELM.

(*Who had gone out, appears excitedly at the door on the right and calls softly.*) Major, Major!

MAJOR (*springing up*).

What is it?

[76]

FRITZCHEN

WILHELM (*in a whisper*).

The—the—young—master!

FRAU VON DROSSE (*turning round suddenly*).

What is it about the young master?

MAJOR (*rushes out. His voice is heard*).

Boy, boy, boy!

(FRAU VON DROSSE *breaks out in ecstatic laughter.*)

AGNES.

Quietly, aunt! Quietly! Don't excite yourself!

SEVENTH SCENE.

THE SAME. FRITZ VON DROSSE (*in hussar uniform, his mother's son, slender, delicate, very youthful, blond to the roots of his closely cropped hair, small curled moustache, erratic person. Uneasiness is veiled beneath a noisy cheerfulness*).

FRAU VON DROSSE.

(*Goes to meet him with outstretched arms.*) My God! there he really is!

FRITZ.

I should think he was! (*Presses her to his heart and strokes her hair, closes his eyes a moment, as if overcome*

[77]

with faintness.)   But be seated, mamma, be seated.   Confound it, but I have ridden!   And on the way, my horse lost another shoe.

MAJOR.

Mohammed?

FRITZ.

No, I am riding the Spy.

MAJOR.

Where did it happen?

FRITZ.

Thank God! just near Gehlsdorf. . . . I wasted twenty-five minutes at the blacksmith's. . . . But then— when—you should have seen! . . . Yes, Wilhelm, just see to it that the horse is well scraped and rubbed down. And don't let him stand just now—first lead him about properly. . . . An hour, feeding time—understand, old chap? . . . There, give me your paw—so!—don't be so agitated. . . . And now, go on, out with you!

(*Exit* WILHELM.)

FRAU VON DROSSE.

Come here, my Fritzchen, sit beside me!

FRITZ.

Very well, mamma, let us, very well!

FRITZCHEN

FRAU VON DROSSE.

You see, Agnes she had a presentiment about you.

FRITZ.

Ah! Good-day, Agnes!

AGNES.

Good-day, Fritz!

FRITZ.

You are so formal!

AGNES.

I? . . . Ah, no, dear Fritz. . . . Would you not like to drink something?

(FRITZ *stares at her, without replying.*)

MAJOR.

Fritz!

FRITZ (*starting up*).

Yes, father!

MAJOR.

You are asked a question.

FRITZ.

To be sure, pardon me! . . . Pardon me, dear Agnes! . . It is the heat . . . It makes one quite idiotic. . . . Please bring me anything you like. . . . No, bring me rather some Rhine wine. . . . Bring some of the '64.

MAJOR (*laughing*).

You go eagerly at the stuff, my son. . . .

FRITZ.

Forgive me, father, if I was too bold.   I don't know how I came to do it.

MAJOR (*to* AGNES).

Just bring it, bring it.

(AGNES *takes the keys from the shelf and goes out to the right.*)

FRAU VON DROSSE.

How long have you furlough, my boy?

FRITZ.

Furlough?   Ha, ha, furlough . . . No furlough at all. Sixty precious minutes, I have spared for you (*stretching himself*) then it is over!   (*Throws himself into a chair standing near the place where his mother is sitting.*)

MAJOR.

It is "over," what does that mean?   Are you then on duty?

FRITZ.

On duty? . . . Well, yes indeed, I am on duty—to be sure—of course.

FRITZCHEN

MAJOR.

What duty can that be?

FRITZ.

Well, a patrol ride, of course.

MAJOR.

When did you set out?

FRITZ.

At noon, father.

MAJOR.

Remarkable. In my time, the cavalry rode in patrol service rather about midnight.

FRITZ.

Yes, the old man* does such things. . . . It is all one to him. If he can give petty annoyance. Yes.

MAJOR.

How do you have time to stop in here?

FRITZ.

Well, I had to unsaddle, and anyhow have ridden four and a half miles. It was only the question whether I should feed the horse at Braun's—at the entrance where one gets merely water or——

* The colonel.

FRITZCHEN

MAJOR.

Of course you are right about that.

FRAU VON DROSSE (*stroking his hands*).

See what brown hands the boy has got. . . . I wonder how they can be burned through the gloves . . . Just look, Richard, he has the white mark on his forehead, there where it is shaded. The last time, it was not there. My boy, my boy! (*Bends down her head and kisses him on the forehead.*)

(*FRITZ closes his eyes and utters a low whimpering exclamation of pain.*)

FRAU VON DROSSE.

What was it? Did I hurt you, my boy?

FRITZ (*with embarrassed laughter*).

Oh, no—no!

MAJOR.

Control yourself, Fritz!

FRITZ.

Yes, father!

FRAU VON DROSSE.

Let him alone, Richard! Remember he has to leave directly.

FRITZ (*staring straight before him*).

Yes, I must go directly.

MAJOR (*shaking his head, examines him*).

Remarkable!

AGNES (*who returns with a bottle and glasses*).

There is the wine, dear Fritz.

FRITZ.

Ah, if only the wine is there! (*Hurries to the table and pours the wine.*)   Does no one touch glasses with me?

MAJOR.

Just wait, I will touch glasses with you.

FRITZ.

Then long life to us, friends!   May we live happily. . . . Long may we live. . . . (*Musing.*)   May we live as long as possible!

MAJOR.

But you are not drinking.

FRITZ.

Yes, yes.   (*Tosses down a glass.*)

MAJOR.

Well, I should like to take this occasion to ask you just why you don't write to us any more.

FRITZCHEN

FRAU VON DROSSE.

Please, Richard, please say nothing to him—he telegraphed.

FRITZ (*starting anxiously*).

Telegraphed? What did I telegraph?

(MAJOR *makes signals to him behind his mother's back*.)

FRITZ.

Yes, of course. You see, father, I telegraphed. . . . And then, not long ago, I fell from the trapeze and sprained my arm a bit.

FRAU VON DROSSE.

You see, Richard, that is what hurt him just now; and yet you scolded him.

FRITZ.

Mamma, father is right. . . . A soldier is not allowed to show signs of pain—he has no pain. That is something which doesn't happen, it is something which doesn't happen at all, does it, Agnes?

AGNES.

Why do you ask *me*, Fritz?

MAJOR.

Remarkable! . . . You know, darling, the boy would like something to eat. In such cases, you always see to it yourself—eh?

[84]

FRITZCHEN

FRITZ.

No, indeed, mother—stay here, mother. (*He grasps her hands.*)

FRAU VON DROSSE (*imploringly*).

Richard, the time is just now so short.

MAJOR.

Won't do, child! I have to speak to him about something.

FRITZ.

What is it, father? There is indeed no question of . . .

FRAU VON DROSSE (*standing up and sighing*).

Don't be too long, Richard. Remember I wish to have something more of him. (*Goes with Agnes to the door on the left, where she turns again.*) My boy, don't you look at me any more?

FRITZ.

(*Who has been standing with averted face, biting his lips, turns suddenly.*) At your service, mother!

FRAU VON DROSSE.

Now he is on his "at your service" footing, even with me.

(*Exit* FRAU VON DROSSE *with* AGNES.)

FRITZCHEN

EIGHTH SCENE.

MAJOR.　FRITZ.

MAJOR.

Well, Fritz, my boy, here we are now alone, just out with what you have to say . . . Exactly what is the matter?

FRITZ.

Nothing, father, absolutely nothing . . . What should be the matter?

MAJOR.

You know, this story about the sprained arm and the patrol ride, that is simply a lie!

FRITZ.

How so?

MAJOR.

Will you smoke a cigar with me?

FRITZ.

If you please . . . That is, I should like a glass of water. (*Tosses down two glasses of water.*)

MAJOR (*lights his cigar*).

Just see, Fritz, in your rage you fail to notice that I am insulting you here.

[86]

FRITZCHEN

FRITZ.

How can a father be said to insult his son? If you don't believe me, then you just don't believe me.

MAJOR.

But we are both officers, my son. . . . Well, let us set that aside—besides that, we are a couple of good friends from time immemorial. . . . Isn't that the case—are we not?

FRITZ.

Oh, to be sure.

MAJOR.

And when I see you running about here—in ecstasy or despair—I can make nothing out of it. Yes, I should like to advise you to put a little more confidence in me. . . . The affair is surely not so bad that a man of experience cannot put it in order again. . . . So just sit down here a while. . . . Have you gambled?

FRITZ.

Yes, I have gambled too.

MAJOR.

Have you lost?

FRITZ.

No, I have won.

FRITZCHEN

MAJOR.

Then, as to women—how is it about women?

FRITZ (*shrugs his shoulders*).

Ah!

MAJOR.

Boy, don't be so hard in the mouth. . . . Do you think I don't know you are in love? . . .

FRITZ.

In love? Ah, good God!

MAJOR.

Just think, my boy, only a year and a half ago, you came to me one fine day and explained to me that you wished to engage yourself to Agnes. . . . You know that I have not the slightest objection to Agnes. She will make an excellent Frau von Drosse.

FRITZ.

Indeed? Do you believe it?

MAJOR.

But your twenty-one years and, ah, good God! . . . You still carry about with you most merrily the egg-shells on your back—as the infantry carries the knapsack. You hadn't the slightest idea of what are commonly called "women"—of course, I don't count barmaids and such people. . . . So I said to you: "My boy, let this interview be buried—and above all, so far as Agnes is concerned. . . . Do as your father and your grandfather did! Get some experience and—then come again." Don't you remember that?

FRITZ.

I should think I did remember it.

MAJOR (*smiling*).

And now, it seems to me, you *have* had some experience.

FRITZ.

Oh, yes, there is no denying that.

MAJOR (*still smiling*).

You have in the end had a so-called "passion," or are stuck in the middle of it; which of the two I don't know. Yet to judge from the discontinuance of your letters, the latter is the case. . . . Since we are here together as two men, I will not expostulate with you further. . . . You know perhaps the story of that abbé who, in society, once excused the absence of his bishop with the words: "Monseigneur est en retard à cause d'amour." To a certain extent, this holds good in every case. . . . But in spite of that, on your mother's account, don't do it again. That is my advice to you. . . . There! And now we'll enter at once upon the matter itself. . . . Just see, Frau von Lanski is, it will be admitted, a very charming woman, but——

FRITZ (*impetuously*).

Father, how do you come to refer to Frau von Lanski?

MAJOR.

There, there, there, only take it calmly, only take it calmly. . . . I know just what there is to know about such affairs, and I don't by any means wish to pry into your secrets . . . But so far as the grand passion is concerned, be calm. . . . I can cure you again . . . Be quite calm.

FRITZ.

That I can well believe, father, if only you have the time necessary to do it.

MAJOR (*smiling*).

Well, why haven't I?

FRITZ.

Because, in twenty-four hours, I shall be a dead man.

MAJOR.

(*Springing up, and taking him by the shoulder.*) Boy!

FRITZ.

Father, I did not wish to tell anything. I came here only to take farewell of you in silence. But you have drawn it out of me, father.

MAJOR (*flying into a passion*).

So, there's a scandal. . . . You had to carry it to the point of making a scandal—you damned fool! (*More calmly.*) Lanski has challenged you?

(FRITZ *nods assent.*)

MAJOR.

Well, yes—and it is well known—Lanski is a dead shot. He is perhaps the best shot anywhere hereabouts. . . . But still your wrist is in good order. How can one throw the thing away like that? I have fought three duels, and two of them under difficult conditions—eh— and—there, see here! How can one say such a thing? How can one, man?

FRITZ.

Father, the affair at this moment is in such a state that, after all, I don't know whether I shall be granted a duel!

MAJOR (*hoarsely*).

I don't understand that, Fritz.

[91]

Fritz.

Then don't ask me! . . . I can't say it, father. . . . I had rather bite off my tongue. (*Pauses.*)

Major.

(*Goes to the door on the left, opens it, looks out, and closes it again.*) Now speak! (*Wildly.*) Speak or——

Fritz.

For me, father, there is no more any "or." . . . Whether you turn me out or not, it is all the same.

Major (*softly, grinding his teeth*).

Do you wish to drive me mad, boy?

(Fritz *crying out*).

He whipped me—across the courtyard—out into the street—whipped me like a beast!

Major (*after a silence*).

Where was your sabre? You could have run him through.

(Fritz *silent, with downcast eyes.*)

Major.

Where was your sabre, I ask you?

Fritz.

It was—not—at hand, father.

FRITZCHEN

MAJOR.

It was—not—at hand. . . . Hm! . . . Now I understand it all. Surely there is nothing left to wish! And this catastrophe occurred when?

FRITZ.

Yesterday evening, father!

MAJOR.

At what time?

FRITZ.

It was still—daylight!

MAJOR.

Ha, ha!

FRITZ.

Father, only don't laugh! Have pity on me!

MAJOR.

Have you had pity on me? . . . Or on your mother? or on—on. . . . Just look, look about you . . . All that was made for you! . . . All that was waiting for you. . . . For two centuries we Drosses have struggled and scraped together and fought with death and devil— merely for you. . . . The house of Drosse was resting on your two shoulders, my son. . . . And you have let it fall into the mire, and now you would like to be pitied!

[93]

FRITZCHEN

FRITZ.

Dear father, listen. . . . Since you have known it, I am quite calm. . . . What you say is all very true, but I cannot bear the responsibility alone. Listen; when I came to you that time, on account of Agnes, my whole heart was attached to her. So far as I was concerned, other men's wives could go to the devil.

MAJOR.

Did I drive you, then, after other men's wives?

FRITZ.

Yes, father, otherwise what does that mean: "Get some experience, ripen, do as your father and grandfather did"? . . . In the regiment, they still call you the wild Drosse, and tales are still told of your former love adventures. . . . They tell some such stories even of a late date. . . . For my part, I had not the least taste for such diversions. I used to see in every woman who did not belong to me, a sort of holy thing. . . . That may have been a green way of looking at it, but you would have allowed it; and with Agnes, I should have quietly——

MAJOR.

Stop! Have pity! Stop!

FRITZCHEN

FRITZ.

See, now you say to me all at once, "have pity"—
Father, I am a dying man, I did not come here to make
reproaches, but do you make none to me!

MAJOR.

(*Embracing him, and stroking his hair.*) My son—
my all—my boy—I don't permit—I will not——

FRITZ.

Silence, silence, father! Mother should not hear that.

MAJOR.

Yes, forgive me for giving way. It shall not happen
again. . . . So how does the affair stand now?

FRITZ.

I reported myself to the old man, that very night.

MAJOR.

My God! Whatever did the old Frohn say?

FRITZ.

Spare me that, father. . . . Of course, I obtained the
usual furlough at once, until the discharge comes. Well,
that doesn't matter now. . . . It does not last long, thus.
. . . This morning, the court of honor had a sitting.
After my hearing, I rode away at once, so as to lose no

time. I gave Mohammed to Hallerpfort in order to
have him follow me as soon as judgment was pronounced.
He may be here at any moment.

MAJOR.

Why did you summon a court of honor?

FRITZ.

What was I to do, father, after Lanski declared to
those who delivered my challenge that I was no longer—
capable of having satisfaction?

MAJOR.

Ah! I will shoot the dog dead for that.

FRITZ.

Well, I hope they will decide favourably to me.

MAJOR.

If not, the dev— (*Softly.*) And then I will tell you
a couple of measures to take so as to have a steady hand.
Sleep properly, and don't eat a bite, and then tell the
doctor——

FRITZ.

Enough, enough, father, that is of no further use.

MAJOR.

What does that mean? Is it possible that you will—
to Lanski?——

FRITZCHEN

FRITZ.

Lanski will hit me.   Depend upon it. . . .

MAJOR.

Man, are you—are you——?

FRITZ.

Lanski will hit me.   Depend upon it. . . .

MAJOR.

Man, yet have—yet consider——

FRITZ.

I will not, father!   And if you had seen the spectacle which the people of Wartenstein saw yesterday (*shudders*), you would demand nothing more of life for me than a half-respectable death. . . .

MAJOR (*brokenly*).

Perhaps—they will not—grant you—the duel.

FRITZ.

Well, if we have got to that last hope, father, then we are indeed in bad straits. . . . Shall I perhaps open a dram-shop in Chicago, or a cattle business with my paternal capital?   Yes?   Would you have done it?

MAJOR (*perplexed*).

I?

[97]

FRITZCHEN

FRITZ.

Say then—say!

MAJOR (*drawing himself up*).

No! (*Sinks down in his chair.*)

FRITZ.

So you see, father—so or so—your Fritz is done for.

MAJOR (*sunk in gloomy reverie*).

My fault!—my——

NINTH SCENE.

THE SAME. WILHELM. *Afterward* LIEUTENANT VON HALLERPFORT.

FRITZ.

What is it?

WILHELM.

Lieutenant von Hallerpfort wishes to speak to the young master.

FRITZ.

(*Hurrying past him to the door.*) Well?

(*HALLERPFORT shakes hands with him and the MAJOR, and casts a glance at WILHELM, who forthwith disappears.*)

FRITZ.

Well?

FRITZCHEN

HALLERPFORT,

Does your father know?

MAJOR.

Yes, my dear Hallerpfort, I know.—Granted?

HALLERPFORT.

To-morrow morning, half after four o'clock—behind the large drill-ground.

FRITZ.

Thank God!

MAJOR.

Thank God! (*They embrace.*)

FRITZ (*disengaging himself*).

Conditions?

HALLERPFORT.

Fifteen paces—advance—five paces barrier—exchange of shots——

FRITZ.

To a finish?

HALLERPFORT.

To a finish.

FRITZ.

Very well!

[99]

FRITZCHEN

(MAJOR *turns toward the door, and presses his hands to his face.*)

HALLERPFORT (*approaching him*).

Major, as your son's best friend——

MAJOR (*grasping his hands*).

I thank you, my dear Hallerpfort, I thank you. . . . You will ride away at once, will you not?

HALLERPFORT.

Unfortunately we must, Major.

MAJOR.

Then just listen. . . . I will pass the hours until the duel, with my son. . . . That you can understand, can't you? . . . My carriage is hitched up—but I cannot go away with you for fear of making my sick wife uneasy. Wait for me at the end of half an hour in Schrander's inn. . . . Don't fear. We shall be on time. . . .

HALLERPFORT.

It will be as you order, Major.

MAJOR.

And now, courage, Fritz!

FRITZ.

That is understood, father!

MAJOR.

(*Holding open the door on the left, in a different tone.*)
Now, boys, just come quickly in!   Only think, darling——

TENTH SCENE.

THE SAME.   FRAU VON DROSSE.

FRAU VON DROSSE.

Ah—Herr von Hallerpfort! (*He kisses her hand.*)
How does this happen? Two lieutenants in the house
at the same time—if that doesn't bring luck!

FRITZ (*quickly*).

We have orders together, mamma.

HALLERPFORT.

And alas, madam, we have to be off this very minute.

FRAU VON DROSSE.

How is that? Then I don't have my full hour? And
now everything is so beautifully arranged. . . . Fritz, my
dear Hallerpfort—just a bite, won't you? . . . Richard,
dear, come to my aid.

MAJOR.

But, dear child, service is service.

[101]

FRITZCHEN

FRITZ (*with quick decision*).

So, good-bye, mamma!

FRAU VON DROSSE (*embracing him*).

My boy—you will soon have furlough, won't you?

FRITZ.

Yes indeed, mamma! After the manœuvres. Then we are free. Then we will be merry!

FRAU VON DROSSE.

And Hallerpfort is coming with you, isn't he?

HALLERPFORT.

With your permission, madam.

MAJOR (*softly, to* AGNES).

Take leave of him! You will never see him again!

FRITZ.

(*Stretching out his hand cheerfully to her.*) Dear Ag— (*Looks into her face, and understands that she knows. Softly, earnestly.*) Farewell, then.

AGNES.

Farewell, Fritz!

FRITZ.

I love you.

AGNES.

I shall always love you, Fritz!

FRITZ.

Away then, Hallerpfort! Au revoir, papa! Au revoir! Revoir! (*Starts for the door on the right.*)

FRAU VON DROSSE.

Go by the park, boys—there I have you longer in sight.

FRITZ.

Very well, mamma, we will do it! (*Passes with* HAL-
LERPFORT *through the door at the centre; on the terrace, he
turns with a cheerful gesture, and calls once more.*) Au
revoir! (*His voice is still audible.*) Au revoir!

(FRAU VON DROSSE *throws kisses after him, and waves
her handkerchief, then presses her hand wearily to her heart
and sighs heavily.*)

ELEVENTH SCENE.

MAJOR. FRAU VON DROSSE. AGNES.

(AGNES *hurries to her, and leads her to a chair, then
goes over to the* MAJOR, *who, with heaving breast is lost in
thought.*)

FRAU VON DROSSE.

Thank you, my darling!—Already, I am quite well
again! . . . God, the boy! How handsome he looked!

And so brown and so healthy. . . . You see, I saw him exactly like that last night. . . . No, that is no illusion! And I told you how the Emperor led him in among all the generals! And the emperor said— (*More softly, looking far away with a beatific smile.*)   And the Emperor said——

CURTAIN.

III

THE ETERNAL MASCULINE

A PLAY IN ONE ACT

PERSONS

THE QUEEN.

THE MARSHAL.

THE PAINTER.

THE VALET DE CHAMBRE.

THE MARQUIS IN PINK.

THE MARQUIS IN PALE BLUE

THE SLEEPY MAID OF HONOUR.

THE DEAF MAID OF HONOUR.

A CHILD AS CUPID.

Several other Marquises and Maids of Honour.

THE ETERNAL MASCULINE

The scene represents a state apartment in a royal castle. On the left, a throne in baroque style. On the right, in the background a screen with a table and chairs beside it. In the centre, an easel.

FIRST SCENE.

THE QUEEN *in a plaited coronation robe,* on the throne. THE PAINTER *with palette in hand, painting.* A CHILD *as* CUPID, *suspended by the waist, swings on* THE QUEEN'S *left, holding a crown over her head. The background and the right of the stage are occupied by ladies and gentlemen of the court, among them* THE DEAF MAID OF HONOUR, THE SLEEPY MAID OF HONOUR, THE MARQUIS IN PINK, *and* MARQUIS IN PALE BLUE.

SONG OF THE MAIDS OF HONOUR.

(LED BY THE MARQUIS IN PALE BLUE.)

Zephyr rises at the dawn
From the budding pillows of the roses.
Lo, he will cool his hot desire
In the silvery dew,

Since he must console himself
That his dream still fans the flame,
And that Luna's icy kiss
Does but touch his parched mouth.

And Aurora's violet passion
Looks on him with floods of tears.
Ah! What matters Luna's favour?—
She knows not how to kiss.

THE QUEEN (*yawning*).

The pretty verses which you have just sung to sweeten this long posing for me, grieve me slightly. Yet—aside from that—accept my thanks.

THE MARQUIS IN PALE BLUE.

Oh, your Majesty!

THE QUEEN.

Are you a poet, Marquis?

THE MARQUIS IN PALE BLUE.

Oh, your Majesty, up to this time I have not been; but who should not speak in verse where this magic enthrals us, where our hearts are habitually broken, and Cupid himself bears the royal crown?

(CUPID *begins to cry*).

FIRST MAID OF HONOUR.

What is the matter with him?

SECOND MAID OF HONOUR.

Ah, the sweet child!

FIRST MAID OF HONOUR.

Be good! Nice and good! Here is a sweetmeat!

CUPID.

I want to get down! My legs are cold.

THE QUEEN.

Oh, fie! The word offends my ears.

THE MARQUIS IN PINK.

Pardon him, your Majesty, the saucy child surely does not know that in your presence one can speak only of roses, lilies, and such delicate things.

THE QUEEN.

It seems to me that the little fellow lacks education.

THE MARQUIS IN PALE BLUE.

Hereafter, only children from superior families should be chosen for this purpose.

THE QUEEN.

And you, respected artist, have no word to say?

THE ETERNAL MASCULINE

THE PAINTER.

It is not fitting that every one should speak. I am engaged to paint, not to make speeches. Still, may I ask you to send the boy away?

(THE QUEEN *laughing, makes a sign. Two maids of honour set him free.*)

THE MARQUIS IN PINK.

What a way of speaking!

THE MARQUIS IN PALE BLUE.

What a plebeian!

THE MARQUIS IN PINK.

How self-conscious!

THE MARQUIS IN PALE BLUE.

And she dotes on him!

THE QUEEN.

Nay, dear master, speak! For rarely do I have the pleasure of finding my thought sympathetically stimulated by the thought of another. I do so like to think—I like to *feel* perhaps even better—yet these gentlemen talk as if they were in a fever.

THE MARQUISES.

Oh, your Majesty!

[110]

THE ETERNAL MASCULINE

THE QUEEN.

Yes, indeed! Look for the man who without hope of meretricious gain knows how to devote himself faithfully to noble service, and who without honeyed phrases gracefully pursues what is dear to his soul; as for you—you could borrow for yourselves a little of love's fire merely from the confectioner's kitchen.

THE MARQUIS IN PINK.

Oh, that is severe!

THE MARQUIS IN PALE BLUE.

Oh, that is almost deadly!

THE QUEEN.

Then resist, and do not drag along inoffensively the burden, new every day, of my old contempt which I bestow upon you, because it pleases me to, like the ordinance of God. But let him expect my reward who can say worthily and honourably: Behold, oh Queen, I am a man!

THE MARQUIS IN PALE BLUE.

I am one!

THE MARQUIS IN PINK.

So am I!

[111]

THE ETERNAL MASCULINE

THE QUEEN.

I don't think ill of you! I like you. You don't disturb my repose—yet, dear master, what say you to that?

THE PAINTER.

I pray, your Majesty, still a little farther to the right.

THE QUEEN (*smiling*).

And is that all? Does nothing which may occur in this room interest you?

THE PAINTER.

Pardon me, your Majesty, the daylight is scanty, and besides—I am painting.

THE QUEEN.

Look at him! A ray of light is of more value to him than all the foolish, gaudy songs of love. Is it not true? See, his very silence and bow betoken decided resistance.

THE PAINTER.

Madam, forgive me if my words and bearing were an occasion and reason for misunderstanding. I speak now, because you call on me to speak. Every ray of light is a ray of love, and if its portrayer were to shut it out, I should like to know what would remain of this poor art which derives its sublimest power from the sources of desire. If our heart does not tremble in our hand, if into the flood of forms which stream from it, no flash of inner lightning shines, how shall we express in these colours life's image, the storm of the passions, the shy play of slight feeling, the desperate vacillation of exhausted hope, and all the rest of our inner life? In these seven blotched colours (*points to the palette*) where the whole wide universe is portrayed, where if our senses are starving for truth, is phantasy to look for food and deliverance? Yet if we have to speak with wisdom, elegantly and cleverly, then the mysterious volition is silent and the promised land recedes far away from us. Therefore, madam, leave me what belongs to us who are poor, the sacred right to create and to be silent.

THE QUEEN.

You call yourself poor—and yet you are rich. You might be equal to the rulers of this earth. Yet what avails the kingdom of your vision? The splendid gift of confidence is wanting to you.

THE PAINTER.

How, your Majesty?

THE QUEEN.

Like a Harpagon, you guard the treasures of your soul, lest any of your feelings should be stolen. No one risks it—Jean, give me my smelling-bottle.

THE ETERNAL MASCULINE

THE MARQUIS IN PALE BLUE
She inflames him.

THE MARQUIS IN PINK.
On the contrary, she cools him off.

THE MARQUIS IN PALE BLUE.
Just to inflame him anew.

THE MARQUIS IN PINK.
I wonder if she truly loves him?

THE MARQUIS IN PALE BLUE.
At any rate, she wishes to excite him.

THE QUEEN.
There, Jean, *merci.* . . . Yet what was I about to say, has no one seen anything of our Marshal?

THE MARQUIS IN PINK (*softly*).
Is he still missing?

THE MARQUIS IN PALE BLUE.
Why does she want *him*, too?

THE QUEEN.
I really believe the good Marshal is offended. It is three days since I spoke to him graciously at the state reception. . . . That seems long to me.

THE PAINTER (*turning to* THE QUEEN).

Is the Marshal back?   The Marshal here?

THE MARQUIS IN PALE BLUE.

May it please your Majesty, a gentleman of the court
met him to-day. He was standing in a pouring rain,
and trying a new sword.

THE PAINTER (*to himself*).

The Marshal.

THE MARQUIS IN PINK.

(*Half aloud to* THE PAINTER.)   Admit, sir, that his
coming is inconvenient to you?

THE QUEEN.

Do you know him, master?

THE PAINTER.

Your Majesty, I have never seen him.

THE QUEEN.

Yet you would like to make his acquaintance?

THE PAINTER.

That I don't know.

THE MARQUIS IN PINK.

(*Softly to* THE MARQUIS IN PALE BLUE.)   How the
coward betrays himself!

THE ETERNAL MASCULINE

THE PAINTER.

Too often I have heard his name spoken in wonder, here with disfavour, there with enthusiasm, yet always as if a miracle was happening to me, too often for me not to view with apprehension the nearness of this powerful man.

THE MARQUIS IN PINK.

What did I say? He is afraid.

THE MARQUIS IN PALE BLUE.

That is splendid!

THE MARQUIS IN PINK.

We must see to that and profit by it. (*Aloud.*) Yet I advise you, dear master, hold your own. He has a habit sometimes of running people through. Yet——

THE PAINTER.

As one impales flies—of an afternoon—on the wall? My felicitations, Marquis! Happily for you, it is plain that he has never been bored.

THE MARQUIS IN PINK.

How do you intend that?

THE QUEEN.

Gentlemen, I must beg you! At court, the master has good company. It amuses me when he meets your insolence with wit and spirit, and gives you a return thrust. Only try the experiment! I am waiting. . . . Please, Jean, my handkerchief!

THE MARQUIS IN PINK.

I have a right to be angry!

THE MARQUIS IN PALE BLUE.

Yes, indeed, you have been insulted!

THE MARQUIS IN PINK.

Ha! Fearful is a man in anger! What do you think— can the dauber defend himself?

THE MARQUIS IN PALE BLUE.

Attack him first from behind, then to his face.

THE QUEEN.

I thank you, Jean. . . . Well, now, you dear men, you whisper, sulk, and mutter to each other. What is the use of my kindling your wit? I don't strike even a little spark from the stone. So you are dismissed. . . . Take a holiday. And do you, my children, go home. But in a little while, master, let us talk together, after our hearts' desire! The ladies of the suite—they will not disturb you.

THE MARQUIS IN PINK.

I believe it. One of them is asleep.

THE ETERNAL MASCULINE

THE MARQUIS IN PALE BLUE.
The other can't hear.

THE QUEEN.
Good-bye! I wish you to go home to do penance for your sins of love. (*Goes to the door on the right.*) One thing more. When you see the good Marshal, give him my greetings. (*Exit, followed by the ladies. Only the sleepy lady remains, sitting.*)

THE MARQUIS IN PALE BLUE.
(*Softly to the deaf lady.*) Pst! Wake her! (*She nods to him pleasantly and goes out.*) Ah, yes, she is deaf!

THE MARQUIS IN PINK.
(*Pointing at the lady asleep.*) Pluck her by the sleeve.

THE MARQUIS IN PALE BLUE.
Fräulein, allow me?

THE SLEEPY MAID OF HONOUR.
(*Springs up with a little cry, makes a low curtsey to* THE MARQUIS, *which he returns in kind, then follows the other ladies.*)

THE ETERNAL MASCULINE

SECOND SCENE.

THE MARQUISES.   THE PAINTER.

(THE PAINTER *paints, without noticing the others, then takes a buttered roll from his pocket and eats.*)

THE MARQUIS IN PINK.

Ha, now I am going to kill him!

THE MARQUIS IN PALE BLUE.

Don't you know it is forbidden? The punishment would be severe. They say, too, that he wields a keen blade, and before you know it you are dead as a mouse.

THE MARQUIS IN PINK.

I am surprised at that. Yet whether we love or hate him, one thing is as clear to me as day: he must not be allowed to quit this palace alive.

ANOTHER MARQUIS.

Pardon me, Marquis, why not?

THE MARQUIS IN PINK.

You don't see deeply into this, Marquis. It seems almost as if you were a simpleton. Has she not mocked us, and exclaimed at our cooing, rustling, sweet speaking, and whimpering? Yet she delights to have him paint her; and as a reward, she loves him.

THE SECOND MARQUIS.

Ha, terrible!

THE THIRD MARQUIS.

Who told you that?

THE MARQUIS IN PALE BLUE.

Have pity on us, friend, and give us proofs!

THE MARQUIS IN PINK.

Well, his Majesty (*all bow*) is, alas, well on in years! (*All assent sorrowfully.*) Whom else does she love? There must at any rate be some one!

THE MARQUIS IN PALE BLUE.

For God's sake, be prudent and speak softly!

THE MARQUIS IN PINK.

What is he doing there?

THE SECOND MARQUIS.

He is eating.

THE MARQUIS IN PINK.

Fie, how vulgar!

THE MARQUIS IN PALE BLUE.

What will happen to the Marshal?

THE ETERNAL MASCULINE

THE MARQUIS IN PINK.

That seems to me doubtful. Sometimes she is pleasant with him, sometimes ill-humoured. I have tried to get rid of him, but he still stays by me. He causes me the pangs of jealousy. She must love one of us. We are here for that purpose. Yet inasmuch as this wandering fellow has stolen her heart, he must die—and that on the spot.

THE MARQUIS IN PALE BLUE.

Patience, Marquis, patience! Of all the means of shaking off this insolent fellow, there is one which is really exquisite. Without breaking the laws, if we set the Marshal on him, instead of being disturbers of the peace, we shall escape scot-free. He dies, of course, and it would be a wonder—yet what am I saying?—He is already as good as a dead sparrow.

(*All chuckle.*)

THE MARQUIS IN PINK.

Dead sparrow is excellent!

THE MARQUIS IN PALE BLUE.

This murder—listen—is bound to put the other one into disfavour. The King's Majesty (*all bow*) will shorten his leave of absence, and we, we shall be freed of him.

(*All chuckle.*)

[121]

THE ETERNAL MASCULINE

THE PAINTER.

What are they about? Alas, if they are glad, perhaps
that means the ruin of some man of honour. Perhaps
they are meditating some ribaldry. But in truth, what
matters to me this vermin?

THE MARQUIS IN PALE BLUE.

Now let us send out a message hastily to the Marshal,
that we are gathered in the antechamber, and while this
poor dead mouse—no, pardon me sparrow!—stammers
his love to her, he, driven by us to extremes, will burst
in unannounced—and this fellow is detected.

THE MARQUIS IN PINK.

Very good! But if things turn out differently, what
then?

THE MARQUIS IN PALE BLUE.

Never mind! Take advantage of the right moment.
No more is needed. For she cannot refrain, she must
see people kneel to her.

THE MARQUIS IN PINK.

Famous! Brilliant! A splendid plan! (*To* THE
PAINTER, *with a low bow which all imitate.*) Honoured
sir, permit us to greet you!

THE ETERNAL MASCULINE

THE PAINTER (*very politely*).

My greeting implies the esteem of which you are aware.

THE MARQUIS IN PALE BLUE.

We lay our esteem at your feet! (*After further bows, which* THE PAINTER *good-humouredly returns*, THE MARQUISES *depart at the centre.*)

(THE PAINTER *smiling, continues to paint.*)

THIRD SCENE.

THE PAINTER. THE VALET DE CHAMBRE. *Then* THE DEAF MAID OF HONOUR. THE SLEEPY MAID OF HONOUR. THE QUEEN.

(THE VALET *entering from the left, greets* THE PAINTER *with condescending nods, and walks over to the throne.*)

THE PAINTER.

Eh!—what? . . . Ah, indeed! (*Laughs aloud.*) Strange world, where the lackey carries his head the highest!

(VALET *after arranging the cushions, places himself before the easel, and ogles the portrait.*)

THE PAINTER.

What is it?

THE ETERNAL MASCULINE

The Valet.

(*Pleasantly, as a connoisseur.*)   Ah—these little furrows in the cheeks! (*Benevolently.*) It can't be expected, sir, of you that your brush should do justice to every fine point. Yet—aside from that—the likeness is good.

The Painter (*laughing heartily*).

Indeed?

The Valet.

(*Opening the door on the left, announces.*) Her Majesty!

The Painter.

I scent trouble in this, and a voice says to me flee! I have already committed many a folly, but I never loved a queen! Take heed to yourself!

(The Two Maids of Honour *have entered during this soliloquy, and have taken their positions to the right and left of the door.*)

The Queen.

(*Nods cordially to* The Painter, *and takes her seat on the throne, as before.*) My dear Jean, I must dispense with you now.   Don't stay too late.

(*Exit Jean.*)

[124]

FOURTH SCENE.

THE QUEEN. THE PAINTER. THE DEAF MAID OF HONOUR (*who seats herself behind the screen*). THE SLEEPY MAID OF HONOUR (*who falls asleep directly on a chair near the door on the left*).

THE QUEEN.

Well, master, tell me: what is Genius doing?

THE PAINTER.

Oh, your Majesty, he is pursuing Beauty.

THE QUEEN.

Yet since Beauty lingers no more on earth, your genius will soon grow weary.

THE PAINTER.

How so? Does your Majesty think it roams in the sky? It lingers just at the goal and cries: Oh behold! and what thou beholdest, that give to eternity!

THE QUEEN.

I did not know, my dear master, that you were so ready with your compliments. Very well! As a man of many travels and of great reputation, you tread continually on the scorn of men; and since we are here chatting in

[125]

confidence, take heart and tell me without reserve, tell me quite frankly: am I really beautiful?

THE PAINTER.

If I were to speak as a man, every word would be presumptuous. Yet you ask the painter only. And he says that his hand is withered with anxiety lest on this canvas there will be found only a pale blotted vapour seen by a blind man.

THE QUEEN.

There spoke the painter. But what says the man?

THE PAINTER.

He has no opinion, your Majesty!

THE QUEEN.

What a pity! One hears now and then this thing and that thing, yet that seems to me insipid above all things. And one must be strict and always be suppressing—suppressing. You don't need that. So I tell you discreetly, I can't resist the suspicion that my beauty is leaving me. Yes, indeed. And besides that, I am growing old. Yes, indeed. I am almost thirty, and the matron has to go to the rear. I indeed do what I can. They take great pains with me. And my late brother used to send me a beauty powder from the holy sepulchre which was good for my complexion. Then it is my habit to wash myself with the extract of lilies, and off and on to nibble at arsenic bonbons. That is very good—the eyes flash, and the blood comes to the cheeks. . . . (*Alarmed.*) It seems to me I am confiding in you.

THE PAINTER.

Consider me as a thing—as a slave!

THE QUEEN.

And you know how to be silent? Tell me—swear!

THE PAINTER.

What you did not will me to hear, that I have not heard. What I did not hear, I cannot keep as a secret.

THE QUEEN.

Lofty sentiment and noble will find expression in you. So, in all silence, I may show your heart what favours are granted to you.

THE PAINTER (*tremulously*).

Am I worth it? And if you regret it to-morrow?

THE QUEEN.

I do not know a to-morrow nor a to-day. My weary sense with crippled wing never strays into the far future, for ah! I, poor, poor Queen, suffer from intense melancholy. I have too much feeling. I have told you that already, and then I am tired of my throne in this world of dreary elegance, where——

THE PAINTER.

Your Majesty! Remember the ladies there!

THE QUEEN.

Ah, the ladies! No chance favours me. That you have perceived already. Yet there is no question of the ladies. One doesn't hear a word; the other sleeps, even while standing up.

THE PAINTER.

Sure enough. . . . Yet when I consider——

THE QUEEN.

Consider nothing. . . . Give me only a consoling word, which in the sultriness of this perverted nature may penetrate my soul like a breath from the forest. You are a man!

THE PAINTER (*laughing to himself*).

Who has lost his head!

THE QUEEN.

So I saw him in my dreams. I feel, too, that you could quite overflow, and I am a little afraid of it.

THE ETERNAL MASCULINE

THE PAINTER.

(*Controlling himself with difficulty.*)   Oh, fear nothing. I know very well the barrier between me and the height of your throne.   Not a desire, not a thought, rises to you.

THE QUEEN.

And yet you think that I am beautiful?

THE PAINTER (*impulsively*).

Yes, you are beautiful! You—(*restraining himself*). Your Majesty, I beg you to turn a little more to the left.

THE QUEEN.

(*Turns her head quite to the left.*)   So?

THE PAINTER.

Yes.

THE QUEEN.

What are you painting now?

THE PAINTER.

Your hand.

THE QUEEN (*pointing to her face*).

And it is for that, that I am to turn to the left?

THE PAINTER.

I meant, just to the centre.

[129]

THE QUEEN.

Is the hand well posed?

THE PAINTER.

Very well.

THE QUEEN.

Can you see it from where you sit?

THE PAINTER.

No, yes—(*she laughs*). Forgive me if I am talking nonsense.

THE QUEEN (*spreading out her hand*).

Here you have it! How the sapphire sparkles! A beautiful stone! . . . You praised my face, but yet you don't say whether you like my hand.

THE PAINTER.

Instead of finding fault with me, look! I have painted it.

THE QUEEN (*pouting*).

You have indeed painted it, but you have not kissed it. From that I conclude that it is not attractive.

THE PAINTER.

And forgive me, if I transgress the rules of your court, more from shyness than from want of intelligence. Even so, the sailor knows well the laws of the stars' movements and yet must often sail a false course.

THE ETERNAL MASCULINE

THE QUEEN.

It seems as if you wished to avoid the subject. I was speaking of a hand—you speak of stars.

THE PAINTER.

You were speaking of *your* hand and that is so far from me that even the eternal will, the might which compels the starry heaven, brings it not one inch nearer to me.

THE QUEEN.

Indeed, do you believe that? (*She rises and goes to the easel.*) Now pray what happened? You willed nothing and compelled nothing, yet please observe—the hand is there.

THE PAINTER.

Madam, where others fell down before you, here it is my duty to warn you. I am not a simple shepherd, and never do I let people make game of me.

THE QUEEN.

Ah, now it becomes interesting! You look at me as savagely as if a hatred quite unappeased and unappeasable possessed you.

THE PAINTER.

A hatred? No, what I laughingly veiled from you was not hatred, no—yet *if* I hate, I hate myself, because, dazzled with splendour, like a drowning man I grasp at the little words which you mockingly deal out to me; because, after the manner of a venal courtier, I quite forgot the pride of the man, and by your favour ate sweetmeats greedily from these hands! Yes, just show them—the white .iry hands laden with the splendid tokens of love: yet stop—think of the end, by the holy God—I recognise myself no more.

The Queen.

Never yet did I hear such words.

The Painter.

When did you ever bow yourself to force? When did passion build you a throne on the ruins of the universe, the only throne to win which is more than an idle pastime, on which in splendid grandeur, instead of all the queens, sits Woman! And if a drone playing in colours ever indeed won a smile from you, take from me but your crown, for I, oh Queen, am—a man!

The Queen.

(*Shrinking back to the throne.*) Enough, I should not listen to you any longer.

The Painter.

You must. You have so willed it.

THE QUEEN.

I will beg you, sir, I will conjure you.

THE PAINTER.

Too late. You offered me love's pay as you would throw a gold piece into the cap of a beggar crouching in the street, and if I, thrilled now by hot desire, employ the only moment of life which commits you into my hands, I will not have you play with me any longer. I will, and you—you—must—before this throne our alliance is ratified. Take away the hand. That, others may kiss, but I, Queen, will have the mouth. I will——

FIFTH SCENE.

THE SAME. THE MARSHAL.

THE QUEEN.

(*Who until now has listened, anxious but not altogether unfriendly, collects herself, and draws herself up in sudden anger.*) I deliver this insolent fellow to you, Marshal. Deal with him as he deserves. (*She goes to the door. There she stops, and gives* THE SLEEPY MAID OF HONOUR *two angry little blows with her fan. The latter springs up, bows, and goes out gravely behind* THE QUEEN, *with* THE DEAF MAID OF HONOUR, *who has risen.*)

THE ETERNAL MASCULINE

SIXTH SCENE.

THE MARSHAL.   THE PAINTER.

THE MARSHAL.

Sir, if you wish to say a paternoster, make haste with it.

THE PAINTER.

Your magnanimity affects me deeply, Marshal. But my soul carries light baggage. Even so, it will journey to heaven. And instead of a last testament, I present this portrait to you, so that, in the confusion, no serious danger may happen to it.

THE MARSHAL.

By your will, it has become mine, and I will gladly keep it. So, draw your sword!

THE PAINTER.

I, sir?

THE MARSHAL.

So, draw!

THE PAINTER.

No, that you will never live to see!

THE MARSHAL.

Then why do you wear a sword?

[134]

THE PAINTER.

Because I choose to.

THE MARSHAL.

You are a coward.

THE PAINTER.

(*Controlling himself, with a smiling bow.*) And you are a hero! (*In the meanwhile the door at the centre is opened.* THE MARQUISES *put their heads in, listening.* THE PAINTER *observes it and takes his sword from the table where he has just laid it.*) See! As the traveller uses the staff to defend himself against dogs, so I must wield it. Such people are to be found at all doors where small men work and lie in wait and play the parasite. (THE MARQUISES *draw back. The door at the centre is suddenly closed.*) Yet ever to bare the sword against you, with whom, out of a timid trustfulness, a bond, a splendid bond of pride, entwined me; whom of all the incompletely great men, I admiringly called the only great man—if ever I were to be guilty of such ignominy, I should not find my small share of peace even in the shade of the most beautiful church-yard lindens.

THE MARSHAL.

Are you still young?

THE ETERNAL MASCULINE

THE PAINTER.

I am not exactly old, yet my fortune has been so check-ered and various that I joyfully had given seven every-day lives for *one* surfeit of this. And in the end—however one may work and strive, it is man's destiny: he dies of Woman. Therefore, instead of passing away slowly by my own, I will quickly find my end by the wife of another. My chariot of victory stops indeed suddenly. I greet its well-appointed driver—and I greet my judge. Thrust on!

THE MARSHAL.

I may be a judge, but I am not an executioner. So do me the favour——

THE PAINTER.

And fighting, let you run me through? No, Marshal! That I must refuse. See! Each of us two has his art. You employ the sword, I the palette. How would it be if I should say to you now in accordance with the practice of my craft: Come, we will paint on a wager? And you do not know the merest precept of light-value, azure, modelling. Very well, you are a dead man for me. After-ward you might—that is allowed you—come to life into the bargain, if you liked.

THE MARSHAL.

You are mocking me, surely!

THE ETERNAL MASCULINE

THE PAINTER.

Surely, no! Yet every fight should be a fight on a wager. Because in a fight between men you are a complete man, I should like to show that I too can do something. You are laughing.

THE MARSHAL.

One who is so nimble with his tongue has, it is said, a sure hand. Perhaps, too, many a device unknown to me is concealed in the wielding of your sword. So be quick, I pray you. I hear the sound of footsteps. Do you stare at me in silence?

THE PAINTER.

Still a little farther to the right!

THE MARSHAL.

What does that mean?

THE PAINTER.

So!—And that may not be looked at, because one is mouldering away! I cannot get over it. Never yet have I found lines like those, never yet a working so gloriously true in the frontal plexus of veins, in the eyebrows, as if one by pure will became a giant. The body delicate—the cheeks thin; for Nature when she fashions her best, makes no boast of vigorous strength. . . . The wish overpowers me—Before I die, sir, I must paint you.

The Marshal.

You seem altogether mad.

The Painter.

I beg you to grant me a respite. I shall be glad to let you kill me, yet only after your portrait is finished.

The Marshal.

And by your creation, you hope to obtain all manner of favour, and quietly to escape. You are cunning indeed.

The Painter.

It is the peculiar pleasure of magnanimity to suspect the magnanimity of others.

The Marshal.

Are you reading me a lecture?

The Painter.

It seems that I must. I must make an effort to win your heart's esteem, which is worth more to me than any amount of foolish play with briskly wielded swords.

The Marshal.

By heaven, sir, you risk a great deal!

THE ETERNAL MASCULINE

THE PAINTER.

I risk nothing. I am a man of death. The world lies behind me—a many-colored picture which God has bestrewed with crumbs of white bread, where each one snatches up and devours and yet does not satisfy his appetite. Only in intoxication can a child of fortune know how the flowers beneath bloom and wither. I have been able to, and my soul with every new work drank to satiety. What matters it if life has deceived me? I asked nothing of it—that was my strength. You see I am pronouncing my obituary. Yet I depart gladly. . . . Already the new host approaches and swarms for me in forests and on plains: What matters it that this hand was mortal; for the portraying is as eternal as the image.

THE MARSHAL.

You are mistaken. Only the deed is eternal. If with bloody sword it did not teach mankind to remember, I should perish like a seed sown by the wind.

THE PAINTER.

It is you who are mistaken, sir. Not your deed has life. It soon follows you into the grave. The portrait of the dead which we give to posterity, in song and form, in parchment and stone, this it is which belongs to immortality. By this you shall be hereafter loved and hated.—

[139]

So even if Achilles destroys the whole world, he has but to let Homer live.

THE MARSHAL.

And so I, you? Yet no song tells us that Homer ever kneeled before Helen.

THE PAINTER.

Not that. But every child knows why: the poor singer was blind.

THE MARSHAL.

Your brush, alas, will not help you at all. Yet I should be well disposed toward you. For he who in death seems to remain a trifler, has taken life in earnest.

THE PAINTER.

That is true.

THE MARSHAL.

I am sorry for you.

THE PAINTER.

Without cause, I assure you!

THE MARSHAL.

And why could you not be silent? How did you so dare, contrary to good reason to climb to your Queen? Did nothing within you say: this is a crime?

[140]

THE ETERNAL MASCULINE

THE PAINTER.

You call it crime—I call it folly!

THE MARSHAL.

Do you pursue your secret pleasures, then, like a sly, cold-hearted thief? The one thing fails which spoke in your favour, the almighty love which disturbs the brain!

THE PAINTER.

Marshal, see, love is a tribute which we piously pay to eternal beauty; and since Nature in creative pride has poured it forth out of her fulness, how should we in fretful resignation say: "This one I love—not that one"? In my love, I love only the picture which proceeds from the lap of pure forms; even as this Queen bestows it as a favour, so it sheds its light far and near; and wherever a picture invites me to a banquet, my heart is present without delay.

THE MARSHAL.

Yet I ask you whether *this* picture invited you to a banquet. Speak quickly—by my sword!

THE PAINTER.

You know very well that no gallant man should move an eyelash at such a question.

THE ETERNAL MASCULINE

THE MARSHAL.

You do not love her—only like a faun you make bold to court her madly. (*Taking hold of him.*) But I love her, and for this reason, you must die.

THE PAINTER.

Forgive me if I am surprised at your logic. It is a great honour for me to know whom you love; moreover, you have already told me repeatedly that I must die; yet that you are confused as to this—is—indeed—only—temper. And see, it is but proper that you love her. The contrary—according to court manners and practice—would be unnatural. Yet the more important question seems to be: does she love you? You look away. Very well, I will tell you. She has met you with smiles and furtive questions, with sweet glances, half longingly, has promised you a thousand delights and gradually has subdued you and your obstinacy. Yet if it involved keeping her promises, she would understand how to wrap herself in her innocence.——It was so—was it not? You are silent, because you are ashamed of the game. Pardon me, sir, if I irritate your wounds.

THE MARSHAL.

It seems you set spies at the door!

THE ETERNAL MASCULINE

THE PAINTER.

Why spies? Eve's old practice, that, Marshal, I know
well. Yet what lies behind it, whether true love or not,
for you or me, cannot be deciphered. If I should survive
the duel, she would probably love *me:* yet because it is
decreed that by your arm, you should be the victor in this
absurd quarrel, she will love you, Marshal. Where
woman's glory rules the world, that is the law—so says
natural history. Do you say nothing?

THE MARSHAL.

A poison is distilled from your words which eats into
the very marrow of my soul.

THE PAINTER.

Only the truth! I swear it, I promise it! And since
against my wish I am still very much alive, because of
your favour, be of use to me, sir, in an experiment.

THE MARSHAL.

Explain yourself!

THE PAINTER.

In order to know exactly how you are thought of in the
highest place, you must perish in the duel.

THE MARSHAL.

In the duel?

THE PAINTER.

Understand me rightly: only in appearance.

THE MARSHAL.

And my reputation as a swordsman goes with it into the bargain.

THE PAINTER.

Oh, not at all! You will get up again.

THE MARSHAL (*laughing*).

My friend, I am not sorry that you are still alive. I have become reconciled with you, and I who have dared a great deal in toil and strife, am astonished at the extent of your courage. Very well, what your cunning mind has devised for your escape, I accept. Yet woe to you if this time you do not win! And now to the work!

THE PAINTER.

Come on! . . . Yet no, by your leave! So that they may believe the incredible about me, I will arrange the thing in naturalistic fashion. (*He draws his sword.*) Is the door locked? (*He walks to the door at the centre, and points his sword at the keyhole.*) Eyes away! I am going to thrust! (*A scream is uttered in the antechamber.*) And now look out! I am going to mark horrid pools of spilt blood! (*He mixes colours on the palette, and hands the* MARSHAL *his sword.*) Hold it, I beg you. (*He smears the sword blade with his brush.*)

THE MARSHAL.

My blood!

THE PAINTER.

Without doubt! *Merci.* (*Takes back his sword.*) Just one tap upon the breast. Yet in case you wish that I spare the waistcoat?

THE MARSHAL.

By no means! That would be too much loss of blood!

THE PAINTER.

Just as you please. (*He moves the easel and table to one side. Softly.*) And make no mistake, the door will open at the first clash of blades.

THE MARSHAL.

Are you ready?

(THE PAINTER *nods assent. They fence.*)

THE MARSHAL.

Famous. . . . Do you know that feint?

THE PAINTER.

It is a good one, is it not?

THE ETERNAL MASCULINE

THE MARSHAL.

Who taught you that?

THE PAINTER.

And this! . . .

THE MARSHAL.

There you missed the quint.

THE PAINTER.

Damnation! .   .

THE MARSHAL.

Ah, that was admirable!

THE PAINTER.

Yet at painting I do better. . . . Is any one listening?

THE MARSHAL.

They are huddled together in a confused group.

THE PAINTER.

Now, if you please!

THE MARSHAL.

Only be at it!

THE PAINTER.

Be careful of the throne, or you will get a bump if you fall! (*He lunges at* THE MARSHAL, *far under the armpit.* THE MARSHAL *falls.* THE MARQUISES *who are pressing in at the half-open door, draw back in horror.*)

[146]

SEVENTH SCENE.

THE SAME. THE MARQUIS IN PINK. THE MARQUIS
IN PALE BLUE. THE OTHER MARQUISES.

THE PAINTER.

Listen to me, gentlemen! What are you about in
there? Stay and bear witness to what you saw.

THE MARQUIS IN PINK (*approaching timidly*).

We stand benumbed at such a glorious deed.

THE MARQUIS IN PALE BLUE (*likewise*).

And we are almost beside ourself with admiration.

THE MARQUIS IN PINK.

What? Really dead?

THE PAINTER (*tauntingly*).

Sir, you seem to be in doubt?

THE MARQUIS IN PINK.

Oh, dear man, how could you think it? I wished only
to afford myself the rapture of seeing whether you had
altogether freed us.

THE MARQUIS IN PALE BLUE.

Yes, indeed, freed! For even although you hated him,
you can never imagine how, in the chambers of this castle,
he has trodden on our dignity.

THE ETERNAL MASCULINE

THE MARQUIS IN PINK.

He stalked about, puffed up with self-conceit, and when we were rising in the esteem of his or her majesty——

THE MARQUIS IN PALE BLUE.

Then came this man with a couple of new triumphs.

THE PAINTER.

How odious!

THE MARQUIS IN PINK.

If you please, sir, how we have laughed when his dear name rang through all the streets after some brand-new fight! As the clever man is aware, fools advertise fools. And without going too near him, I will——

THE MARSHAL.

There, wait!

(ALL THE MARQUISES *starting with fear.*)

THE MARQUIS IN PINK (*trembling*).

You said?

THE PAINTER.

I said nothing at all.

THE MARQUIS IN PALE BLUE.

Yet plainly——

[148]

THE ETERNAL MASCULINE

THE SAME. THE VALET DE CHAMBRE. THE QUEEN. THE DEAF MAID OF HONOUR. THE SLEEPY MAID OF HONOUR.

THE VALET (*announces*).

Her Majesty!

THE QUEEN.

I heard a rumour which greatly displeased me and troubled my peace of mind extremely. Is it true? . . . There lies the great hero; and truly, in death he seems even more insignificant than he was—as insignificant as one of the most insignificant. Yet mourn with me! We have had a great loss. Even if ambition urge you on with a double spur, many a fine day will come and go before his like will be born to us.

(THE MARSHAL *clears his throat softly.*)

THE QUEEN.

May his courtliness, too, be pleasantly remembered! After his campaign he always brought back to his Queen the best of the splendid spoil of his booty. That touched my royal heart and will be cited as a glorious example. And yet now to you . . . What did they say to me? It sounds almost untrue and unnatural: are you the David

[149]

of our Goliath? I use the term "Goliath" only figuratively. For though we are mourning at his bier, it cannot be said that he was a giant. Yet we know his disposition was haughty. (THE MARQUISES *eagerly assent.*) Surely he broke in upon you in sudden anger? You are silent out of generosity. So I will graciously forgive *this fault* and *another* fault too. (THE PAINTER *clears his throat softly. She stretches out her hand to him, which he kisses.*) And be not grieved! (*To* THE MARQUISES.) Does not what has happened seem almost like a judgment of God?

THE MARQUIS IN PALE BLUE.

It is true! Here a higher power has been at work.

THE DEAF MAID OF HONOUR.

Pardon me, your Majesty! The Marshal is laughing.

THE MARQUISES (*muttering in horror*).

Is he laughing? Is he laughing? (*Silence.*)

THE MARSHAL (*rising*).

Madam, forgive me! In the fight a sudden fainting fit overcame me.

THE MARQUIS IN PALE BLUE.

(*Pointing at* THE PAINTER'S *sword lying on the floor.*) And what is this blood? (*Movement by* THE PAINTER.)

THE ETERNAL MASCULINE

THE MARSHAL.

Until the return to my senses relieved me (*with emphasis*) of *this* trouble and *another* trouble.

THE QUEEN.

(*Quickly collecting herself. Sharply.*) My congratulations, sir! And my sympathy as well! What has happened to you gives me unspeakable distress. The court atmosphere is indeed rather close, and seems insupportable to great conquerors; which often betrays itself in wrong fancies and swoons. Therefore I am obliged to exercise my power as Queen, and protect your good health against danger. Jean, announce me to his Majesty! (*Exit* JEAN *on the left.* THE QUEEN, *punishing* THE PAINTER *with a glance of unspeakable scorn, follows slowly. The two Maids of Honour go after her.*)

NINTH SCENE.

THE MARSHAL. THE PAINTER. THE MARQUISES (*in the background*).

THE MARSHAL.

I thank you, sir! The mists are dissipated. The eye sees clearly once more; the will has a free hand.

THE PAINTER.

But I was silently executed. Did you notice her look?

THE ETERNAL MASCULINE

THE MARSHAL (*pointing at* THE MARQUISES).

Of looks, there are sufficient.

THE PAINTER (*snatching up his sword*).

Oho! I am always expecting foul play.

THE MARSHAL.

For what reason ? Get along with you! Get along with you! Be quick!

THE PAINTER.

It is true. You are right. Here, we are ruined.

THE MARSHAL.

And what is to become of you ?

THE PAINTER.

That has never troubled me. The world is wide. One can walk about it, and find something to sketch by the way.

THE MARSHAL.

How would it be if you went with me ?

THE PAINTER.

Where ?

THE MARSHAL.

To the camp.

[152]

THE ETERNAL MASCULINE

THE PAINTER.

Yes, and what is there?

THE MARSHAL.

Plenty for you! You will find gay fare, and pastimes and diversions. As much as you want.

THE PAINTER.

And are there fights too?

THE MARSHAL.

Indeed, there are!

THE PAINTER.

And will there be a bold reconnoissance by night?

THE MARSHAL.

Often.

THE PAINTER.

Capital! I will ride with you. In my mind's eye I see already golden moonrise, and silver vapour on the dark alder bush. . . . Are there also songs and notes of the mandolin?

THE MARSHAL.

Plenty of them!

THE PAINTER.

Hurrah! There is music too!

[153]

THE ETERNAL MASCULINE

THE MARSHAL.

And in the story-telling by night at the camp-fire many a tale of human destiny will be unfolded to you.

THE PAINTER.

A world of pictures! (*More softly.*) And love adventures?

THE MARSHAL.

If you choose to call them "adventures."

THE PAINTER.

Agreed, sir! And an excess of happiness will flow out of my soul like a prayer.—Yet it seems I am forgetting the greatest happiness. I shall be with you. I may paint you.

THE MARSHAL.

Take care!

TENTH SCENE.

THE SAME. THE VALET DE CHAMBRE. THE QUEEN. THE TWO MAIDS OF HONOUR.

VALET.

Your Majesty!

(THE QUEEN *rustles over from the left to the right, without bestowing a glance on the two men. At the door on the right she gives the* VALET *a scroll with which he advances. Then she goes out, followed by the Maids of Honour.*)

THE ETERNAL MASCULINE

The Marshal.

Now the hastily contrived reward of our misdeeds is at hand. (*To* Jean.) My noble sir, bestir yourself. (*To* The Painter.) That is the handsome Jean as an angel of justice! (*He unfolds the scroll and reads, laughing.*)

The Painter.

And to me, what do you bring to me?

The Valet.

(*With an expression of awkward contempt.*) You?—Nothing!

The Painter.

Exquisite!

The Valet.

But yes! Your reward shall be meted out to you in the office of the Marshal of the court.

The Painter (*amused*).

Indeed?

The Valet.

Yes! (*Behind the scenes on the right are heard cries of "Jean! Jean!"*)

The Deaf Maid of Honour.

(*Hurries in from the right.*) Jean! Have you forgotten her Majesty?

[155]

THE VALET (*sweetly*).

Oh, no! Tell her Majesty I am coming directly.

THE PAINTER AND THE MARSHAL.

(*Look at each other, and break out into laughter.*)

THE MARSHAL.

Look, look, my friend! He seems to have got into bad habits.

THE PAINTER (*pointing at him*).

It is rightly so. I had almost begged him, at the court where we men are forbidden, proudly to represent the eternal masculine. (*Laughing, they both bow to him.*)

(*Exit* THE VALET.)

THE PAINTER.

But we are going into the flowery open, to our merry pursuits.

THE MARSHAL.

And to combat! (*They walk arm in arm, bowing right and left, toward the door, past* THE MARQUISES, *who, without hiding their disrespect, nevertheless recognise them in a not uncourtly fashion.*)

CURTAIN.